# Child Neglect and Behavioural Parent Education

## Research and Practice

**Benny McDaniel**
and
**Karola Dillenburger**

RHP

lishing

First published in 2014 by:
Russell House Publishing Ltd.
58 Broad Street
Lyme Regis
Dorset DT7 3QF

Tel: 01297-443948
Fax: 01297-442722
e-mail: help@russellhouse.co.uk
www.russellhouse.co.uk

British Library Cataloguing-in-publication Data:
A catalogue record for this book is available from the British Library.

ISBN: 978-1-905541-91-1

Typeset by TW Typesetting, Plymouth, Devon
Cover photo: www.dreamstime.com
Printed by IQ Laserpress, Aldershot

**About Russell House Publishing**

Russell House Publishing aims to publish innovative and valuable materials to help managers, practitioners, trainers, educators and students.

Our full catalogue covers: families, children and young people; engagement and inclusion; drink, drugs and mental health; textbooks in youth work and social work; workforce development.

Full details can be found at www.russellhouse.co.uk
and we are pleased to send out information to you by post.
Our contact details are on this page.

**We are always keen to receive feedback on publications and new ideas for future projects.**

# Contents

# Foreword

Child neglect presents as the most common form of child maltreatment which only in recent years has begun to receive more attention by policy makers, researchers and practitioners. It is no longer seen only as omission of children's basic needs, but, due to the accumulative nature of neglect, is now also recognised as commission, if early identification and intervention do not take place. The understanding of this problem now goes beyond physical neglect, to incorporate health, emotional, educational and social areas which often have devastating long-term consequences for a child. This is encouraging.

Having been involved for over 30 years in researching and working with failure-to-thrive children and their families, where neglect and emotional abuse were dominant features, I was very happy to write a foreword to this very useful and well-written book.

*Child Neglect and Behavioural Parent Education: Research and Practice*, by Dr Benny McDaniel and Professor Karola Dillenburger, describes in a very clear way parenting education and skill training that was originally developed for very young and vulnerable single mothers who were undergoing assessment in a Barnardo's Residential Family Centre. When undertaking this work there and elsewhere, the authors use behavioural methods in doing painstaking assessments of each mother and then devise a tailor-made individual parent-training programme to accommodate specific learning needs and skill deficits.

Behavioural methods lend themselves to co-operative goal setting and working together, empowering mothers to take control of their lives as well as take responsibility for the way they parent their children. Of course, there is no single theory or approach that can claim universal success when dealing with multi-variant problems such as neglect. But focussing on a few clearly defined, achievable tasks can go a long way, as demonstrated in this book.

What sets this book apart from others is its careful attention to all training details and to collaborative processes in working with these young and vulnerable mothers. For parent education to be successful requires a good working relationship between the young, inexperienced mother and the practitioner, in which the knowledge and skills of the worker embrace identified maternal strengths and motivation to produce mutually desirable changes. It means that the mother actively participates in the setting of the learning goals and the process of learning.

The authors convincingly demonstrate that such an approach, through the use of behaviour analytic theory and procedures, empowers and motivates the mothers to become better-informed parents. The book describes a range of methods and techniques which have been used, and their effectiveness is demonstrated through individual case studies. It also provides assessment and evaluation tools on feeding, bathing, safety, hygiene, etc., which practitioners and researchers are bound to find useful in their work with neglectful parents.

I believe that this book will provide valuable information for practitioners, policy makers and managers on how to prevent the escalation of neglect, by allocating resources and devising treatment and intervention for vulnerable parents early on, helping them to become better informed, sensitive and responsible parents.

**Professor Dorota Iwaniec**
*Holywood, Co Down*
*October 2013*

# Preface

## The scale of the problem

About half of the children on child protection registers or subject to child protection plans are listed because of neglect or serious concerns about the potential of neglect.

> Last year over 21,000 children in the UK were subject to child protection plans because they were at risk of harm from neglect – up 7.5 per cent on the previous year.
>
> NSPCC, 2012

Yet, child neglect has received much less attention than other forms of maltreatment, such as physical or sexual abuse. There is little empirical evidence on interventions that specifically address neglect or the prevention of neglect.

## The effects of neglect on physical and mental health

Safeguarding children from neglect is a key function of the family, child care workers, educators, and society at large. Child neglect causes untold damage not only for the baby or child at the time, but in the long-term as children grow into adults. Adults who have been neglected as children are often unable to lead happy and fulfilled lives because they may find it difficult to form good relationships and can be prone to develop mental health problems or become involved in the criminal justice system. At a time when evidence-based practice is demanded in all areas of child care and protection, effective strategies for safeguarding children from neglect must be a key focus for research and practice.

Neglect impacts on all areas of children's health and development. In addition to the obvious physical risks that result from poor caretaking practices, such as physical injury due to poor supervision, neglect has adverse effects on children's psychological and emotional wellbeing. Neglected children are likely to present as passive and withdrawn, have complicated attachments, experience cognitive delay, and experience low self-esteem.

## The intention of this book

In this book we build on over 40 years combined experience in research and working directly with children and using behavioural parent education and training to promote child development, care, and education. The research and practice described in this book shows how parents, in particular those who are young and vulnerable, can be educated to ensure that their babies and young children are safe and appropriately cared for. The behaviour analytic parent education and training methods described in this book are not prescriptive, but entail guidance on drawing on a range of techniques including coaching and feedback, video or in-vivo modelling and role play, instruction, rehearsal, and triadic methods that involve the professional, parent and child. They guide child care workers on how to design and evaluate individualised programmes in a context of behavioural parent education. The book outlines the issues and the theory and research underpinning behavioural parent programmes for neglect and shows how evaluation of such programmes in individual circumstances can help make them accountable, transparent and effective in a way that is culturally sensitive, empowers parents and effectively safeguards children from neglect.

This book does not depend on any additional materials and, unlike some commercial parent education packages, is not restricted to specific intervention techniques in particular contexts. The goal is to enable and empower workers and parents, rather than to make them adhere to a fixed programme.

Because it is adaptable, both in agreeing on individual targets and by adapting their application through individual evaluation, the approach can be used with all parents, including those with intellectual disabilities and those who are vulnerable, for a variety of possible reasons, including being young first-time mothers. The programmes will generally need to be supplemented by other services such as individual counselling, learning homemaking skills, and on-going advice and support with child care duties. Individual data collection instruments and assessment checklists are described in detail under each programme with guidance on using them and examples of research findings that show their effectiveness with very young, vulnerable families with children at risk of neglect.

The emphasis in this approach on adaptability means that this book can be used in study and practice throughout the world. Developed by Benny McDaniel while managing a Barnardo's residential family assessment unit in Northern Ireland, and already used within Barnardo's across the UK, it is supported by the work of internationally respected educator and researcher Karola Dillenburger.

## *The advantages of using parent education based on behaviour analysis*

*First*, it offers a transparent way of working that promotes service user involvement and has a comprehensive underpinning knowledge base.

*Second*, expectations of parents are clearly outlined and progress is evidenced.

*Third*, the emphasis on reinforcing parents' strengths rather than focussing on parental deficits create positive collaborative relationships. Rather than assuming that the parent is inadequate or at fault, the emphasis on evaluation in behaviour analysis allows working methods to be adapted quickly to ensure that they are effective in achieving the agreed goals.

Behaviour analytic interventions fit well within an ethical, evidence-based practice paradigm, as they are based on a well-established knowledge base and on methods that have been tested and can be replicated. In particular, the use of single system research designs provides accountability and transparency and facilitates data-based decision making (Keenan & Dillenburger, 2012).

## *The structure of this book*

This book describes how a behaviour analytic knowledge base can inform research and practice to address a wide range of behaviours relevant to safeguarding children from neglect. The first chapter explores the definition and family, child and socio-economic factors of child neglect. The second chapter outlines the basic principles of behaviour analysis. Some of the most common misrepresentations of behaviour analysis are addressed. The third chapter applies behaviour analytic knowledge to child neglect, in particular examining contingencies that lead to and maintain patterns of neglect. Examples of behaviour analytic interventions are discussed. Chapter 4 delineates the issues related to behavioural parent education. This leads on, in Chapter 5, to the development of individual programmes. Chapters 6 to 10 provide examples of individual programmes for families whose children were on the child protection register at risk of neglect. Each programme is linked to specific aspects of parenting, including basic child care skills, child care routines, home safety, home hygiene, and parent child interaction. Chapter 11 outlines the implications of the development and evaluation of these programmes and explores why behavioural parent education is more effective with some families than with others. Finally, recommendations are made for families, professional practice, and policy.

## *Practice Tools*

At the back of the book is a facsimile of the Practice Tools used in the authors' own work at the time of publication.

They include information on how the Practice Tools can be obtained in an adaptable, electronic format.

# Acknowledgements

We want to thank the young mothers and their babies who participated in and contributed to the research, sometimes during very difficult life circumstances. We also want to thank the staff involved for their perseverance and hard work during the development of the programmes. For confidentiality we do not mention any names here, but you know who you are.

We want to dedicate this book to Ross Oliver and Mickey Keenan.

# About the Authors

**Benny McDaniel** is Quality Specialist, working in Colin Early Intervention Community in Belfast, where she is responsible for supporting the implementation and quality assurance of a range of evidence-based early intervention programmes for children and families.

Benny is a qualified social worker with more than 25 years practice and management experience. Benny previously worked in Barnardo's, managing a residential family assessment unit where the material for this book was developed. Since the completion of her PhD in 2003, Benny has worked on service design and evaluation across a range of family and child care services. Benny has published a number of academic peer reviewed papers and has presented her work at numerous local and international conferences.

**Karola Dillenburger** is Professor of Behaviour Analysis and Education and Director of the Centre for Behaviour Analysis at the School of Education at Queen's University Belfast, where she also co-ordinates the MSc in Autism Spectrum Disorders, leads the approved Behaviour Analyst Certification Board (BACB) online course sequence, and supervises many Masters and Doctoral Students. Her research focuses on evidence-based early intervention for vulnerable children, parent education, and parenting across the lifespan.

Professor Dillenburger is a Board Certified Behaviour Analyst-Doctoral (BCBA-D) and has worked extensively in child care, education, and therapeutic settings before being called to Queen's University Belfast. She has published widely, including five paper-copy books and one ibook, five multimedia training resources on DVDs and CD-ROMs, and over 50 academic peer-reviewed papers. She frequently is invited to teach or deliver international keynote addresses in USA, India, Europe, and Australia.

# CHAPTER 1

# Child Neglect

Child neglect continues to be the most prevalent form of child maltreatment, yet it has received less specific research attention than other forms of child abuse. In this chapter, neglect is defined and conceptualised and the prevalence and aetiology of child neglect are described and put in context.

In the USA, more than 3 million child maltreatment reports are made each year (nearly 6 reports per minute) and more than 740,000 children and young people require medical treatment as a result of child abuse each year, costing the State $124 billion each year (CDC, 2012). In the UK, over 21,000 children in the UK are registered to be at risk of harm from neglect (NSPCC, 2012). Yet, it is only relatively recently that neglect has been viewed as a phenomenon that needs to be conceptualised separately to other forms of abuse (Iwaniec, 2006).

While it is clear that neglect is related to the lack of adequate safe child care behaviours, there is still no single agreed definition. It is difficult to come up with a common definition or a single concept because so much depends on individual, cultural and economic values about what constitutes acceptable standards of child care and what role the State should take in enabling parents to maintain these standards.

In the UK, the most commonly used definition of neglect is outlined by the Department of Health (2006: 33):

> Neglect is the persistent failure to meet a child's basic physical and/or psychological needs, likely to result in the serious impairment of the child's health or development. Neglect may occur during pregnancy as a result of maternal substance abuse. Once a child is born, neglect may involve a parent or carer failing to provide adequate food and clothing, shelter including exclusion from home or abandonment, failing to protect a child from physical and emotional harm or danger, failure to ensure adequate supervision including the use of inadequate care-takers, or the failure to ensure access to appropriate medical care or needs treatment. It may also include neglect of, or unresponsiveness to, a child's basic emotional needs.

The definition of child maltreatment in the USA also places responsibility firmly on parents/caregivers but offers a somewhat clearer statement by differentiating between acts of commission or omission. While both result in 'harm, potential for harm, or threat of harm to a child', acts of commission are considered abuse (in other words, physical, sexual, and psychological abuse), while acts of omission are considered neglect (CDC, 2012):

> The failure to provide for a child's basic physical, emotional, or educational needs or to protect a child from harm or potential harm. Like acts of commission, harm to a child may or may not be the intended consequence. The following types of maltreatment involve acts of omission: failure to provide (physical, emotional, medical/dental, and educational neglect), failure to supervise, and exposure to violent environments.

Undoubtedly, these definitions are very limited and open to interpretation. Rather than offering pro-active guidance that is preventative and constructive, these definitions delineate neglect in terms of extreme harm to the child and place responsibility for adequate care solely on the parents' shoulders. Although the CDC (2012) definition addresses the issue of intentionality, both definitions ignore the fact that neglect can occur as a result of risk factors beyond parental control, for example, poverty, poor housing, or inadequate or unsafe play facilities. Furthermore, differences are not addressed between short-term or recent and long-term or chronic neglect, the effects of the latter being much more severe and obviously if not tackled adequately, short-term or recent neglect may be just the beginning of long-term maltreatment.

The purpose of these definitions is to enable professionals and courts to make decisions about legal action as opposed to enabling professionals to decide what supports are necessary. Consequently, decisions regarding interventions remain largely based on professional opinion and resources available. This resources-led approach stands in contrast to a rights-based approach as postulated in the United Nations Convention on the Rights of the Child that views the child as having the right to protection with the role of families as nurturers of children and essentially the Government's role to protect and assist families in fulfilling this role. Table 1:1 delineates some of the most pertinent articles from the UN

**Table 1.1:**   Articles of the UN Convention on the Rights of the Child [CRC] specifically significant for safeguarding children from neglect (UNICEF, 2012: 1–4)

*Article 3 (Best interests of the child):* The best interests of children must be the primary concern in making decisions that may affect them. All adults should do what is best for children. This particularly applies to budget, policy and law makers.

*Article 4 (Protection of rights):* Governments have a responsibility to take all available measures to make sure children's rights are respected, protected and fulfilled. Governments are then obliged to take all necessary steps to ensure that the minimum standards set by the Convention in these areas are being met. They must help families protect children's rights and create an environment where they can grow and reach their potential.

*Article 5 (Parental guidance):* Governments should respect the rights and responsibilities of families to direct and guide their children so that, as they grow, they learn to use their rights properly. The Convention . . . does place on governments the responsibility to protect and assist families in fulfilling their essential role as nurturers of children.

*Article 18 (Parental responsibilities; state assistance):* Both parents share responsibility for bringing up their children, and should always consider what is best for each child. The Convention . . . places a responsibility on governments to provide support services to parents . . .

*Article 19 (Protection from all forms of violence):* Children have the right to be protected from being hurt and mistreated, physically or mentally. Governments should ensure that children are properly cared for and protect them from violence, abuse and neglect by their parents, or anyone else who looks after them.

*Article 24 (Health and health services):* Children have the right to good quality health care – the best health care possible – to safe drinking water, nutritious food, a clean and safe environment, and information to help them stay healthy.

*Article 26 (Social security):* Children – either through their guardians or directly – have the right to help from the government if they are poor or in need.

*Article 27 (Adequate standard of living):* Children have the right to a standard of living that is good enough to meet their physical and mental needs. Governments should help families and guardians who cannot afford to provide this, particularly with regard to food, clothing and housing.

*Article 28 (Right to education):* All children have the right to a primary education, which should be free. Young people should be encouraged to reach the highest level of education of which they are capable.

*Article 31 (Leisure, play and culture):* Children have the right to relax and play, and to join in a wide range of cultural, artistic and other recreational activities.

*Article 36 (Other forms of exploitation):* Children should be protected from any activity that takes advantage of them or could harm their welfare and development.

*Article 39 (Rehabilitation of child victims):* Children who have been neglected, abused or exploited should receive special help to physically and psychologically recover and reintegrate into society. Particular attention should be paid to restoring the health, self-respect and dignity of the child.

Convention on the Rights of the Child [CRC] for the context of prevention of child neglect.

The CRC clearly considers the child's welfare as paramount by placing responsibility on parents/primary caregivers as the main persons responsible to ensure child welfare, nonetheless equally pronounced is the emphasis and importance placed on Governments in supporting parents/caregivers in this role. Yet, the CRC does not prescribe standards of care.

## Standards for parenting

Problems in defining neglect are rooted in the difficulty in agreeing adequate standards of care. This problem arises not only because it is difficult to delineate criteria but also because standards of care are influenced by individual, family, and cultural differences that tend to change across time. For good reason and in line with an anti-discriminatory practice ethos, professionals are wary of imposing their own values on families. In addition of course, standards change according to current scientific, professional, and public awareness about what is harmful for children and neither local laws for safeguarding children nor the UN Convention for the Rights of the Child address the problem of defining adequate parenting standards.

Because of the differences in standards for care across families, cultures and times, child neglect is particularly difficult to detect. For example, there are cultural differences regarding the age at which a child can be left at home alone or at what level of intoxication a parent is unable to care for a child. In addition, different professional groups, such as teachers, child care workers, and health care workers are likely to have differing thresholds in defining neglect. Agreement is reached more easily in severe cases, such as extremely unhygienic living conditions, repeated infections, malnutrition, or failure to thrive and where medical evidence is available.

## Effects of neglect

It can be difficult to demarcate the effects of neglect from those of other kinds of abuse, poverty, and social isolation. Neglect commonly has an effect on the child's physical health that is due to omission rather than active abuse, for example, lack of supervision can lead to accidental injury, falls, foreign bodies inserted in noses or ears, or unhygienic living conditions, can lead to infections, very severe nappy rash, untreated lice infestation, body odour, or unkempt appearance that in turn leads to rejection by peers. In fact, neglect can begin prenatally, if the foetus is exposed prenatally to unhealthy substances such drugs, tobacco or alcohol or extreme physical or psychological stress or nutritional deprivation.

Although most child neglect is not fatal, frequently children die as a result of a single incidence of neglect, for example, when a young child is left unsupervised in a full bath tub or has access to poisonous cleaning materials, matches, or flammable objects. Child fatalities can also be caused by drowning, scalding, house fires, ingestion, choking, being left alone in a car on a hot day, and failure to follow medical instructions. One of the main risk factors for fatal child neglect is the child's age, with younger children more likely to suffer fatal neglect than older children. Also, gender is a risk factor; the number of boys' deaths exceeding girls' by 2:1. It is difficult to predict these fatalities because they occur as a result of single incidents of neglect, rather than long-term neglect. Only about 1/3 of families in which fatal child neglect occurred are known to social or human services, yet neglect (including medical neglect) is responsible for an estimated 34.1% of child maltreatment deaths and is a contributing factor in many more child deaths (Child Welfare Information Gateway, 2012).

Sustained neglect may not be fatal but can have very adverse cumulative effects on physical health, (for example, loss of teeth due to poor dental care), as well as mental health and social development, (for example, low self-esteem, difficulty in trusting others, poor school performance, and problems in interacting with peers). Neglected children are more likely to be easily distracted, passive, unhappy, and disorganised than other children. They are at increased risk of cognitive delays and being unresponsive to caretaking efforts.

In the long term, adults who have suffered child neglect when they were young may have difficulty parenting and sustaining relationships, suffer from mental illness, and experience substance abuse and involvement in criminal activity. Intergenerational transmission of neglect occurs only in a minority of chronically neglecting families, although one research study found that 70% of parents who had experienced abuse or neglect could be classed as having significant parenting problems; 40% of parents who maltreated their children had been maltreated when they were young (Egeland, Bosquet, & Levy Chung, 2002).

One of the main challenges in preventing neglect, is the difficulty in identifying children who are at risk from neglect. Formal risk assessment protocols, such as Parent Assessment Manual Software [PAMS] (2013) or Graded Care Profile (2009) can enhance but not substitute for clinical judgement and take into account a range of variables, including demographic, social, biological, cognitive, and behavioural characteristics of individuals, families and communities. Of course, the presence of risk factors does not automatically mean that children are neglected. Important factors, such as the severity of the neglect, the age and ability of the child, the co-operation of the main caregiver and their intent, as well as previous contact with Social Services should be taken into consideration to ensure that the focus is on the interactional processes rather than merely on individual deficits.

Interventions focus broadly on three levels:

*Primary level* interventions are aimed at the entire populations and involve large-scale programmes to target wide social issues, such as poverty and poor housing.

*Secondary level* interventions are aimed at families at different levels of risk and include day-care programmes for preschool children, home visiting services, practical support, or parent skills training (DePanfilis, 2006).

*Tertiary level* interventions are aimed at building skills and preventing neglect at a family level. They are usually individually tailored programmes ranging from individual and group work with parents to interventions that are directly aimed at children, such as the provision of day care.

Short-term interventions may be effective in acute cases of neglect but most interventions need to be long term, focused and purposeful. Despite considerable effort, most neglect interventions demonstrate limited success with high rates of recidivism (Gershater-Molko et al., 2002) and at times legal intervention is necessary where voluntary intervention is not making progress. In extreme cases, this can include the removal of the child from the family.

## Models and perspectives

One of the reasons why interventions are ineffective is inconsistency in their application. Difficulties arise when professionals are working from different theoretical or practice perspectives and theories. A closer look at the evolution of these models illuminates the problem.

Initially, explanations about the causes of abuse and neglect focused mainly on the individual *medical model* and the influence of *psychoanalytic theories* led to an emphasis on intra-psychic and emotional pathologies rather than external stressors. Consequently, the roots for child maltreatment were sought in parents' psychiatric or pathological defects or disorders, with a particular focus on mothers. Extreme examples contend that women who neglected their children had personality or psychiatric disorders.

*Attachment* has been viewed as necessary for biological, ethological and evolutionary survival based on the idea that the child has a biological pre-disposition to seek proximity to and contact with a caregiver, specifically when frightened, tired or ill and this attachment seeking behaviour is necessary for the survival of the species (Bowlby, 1982). Attachment has been widely assessed using the Strange Situation (Ainsworth & Wittig, 1969) which involves observing a child's behaviour alone, without their main caregiver, while exposed to an unknown person and an unfamiliar setting. The behaviour of the child when reunited with their main caregiver is categorised as indicator of the quality of attachment, in other words, a statement is made regarding their attachment being secure, avoidant, ambivalent/resistant, or disorganised.

Although widely used, the Strange Situation is problematic for a number of reasons.

First, it is not culturally sensitive, in other words, separation from a parent may not have the expected results in cultures where children are rarely separated from their parents, where parents teach children to be separated without distress, for example, through the use of regular child minders, or where children are routinely cared for by an extended group of caring adults, such as Kibbutz-type arrangements.

Second, it places the cause of attachment behaviours inside the child and thus falls prey to mentalism and circular reasoning. Clearly, infant patterns of behaviour are closely related to the behaviour of the attachment figure. The quality of attachment is directly linked to receiving sensitive caregiving, specifically from parents who are able to read and respond appropriately to the child's cues and needs. In attachment theory, children are said to form *internal working models*, based on their experiences of relationships with their main carers, which subsequently influence their ability to form and maintain adult relationships. It is thought that early negative experiences need to be integrated to form a coherent working model of relationships and if this does not happen problems with later relationships may occur. For the behaviour analyst, the concept of 'working models' does not explain why the child may or may not engage in attachment behaviours. In fact, these kinds of mentalistic ideas detract from searching for the real reasons of behaviour. More on this later.

*Bonding* on the other hand is thought to be the extent to which parents feel that their child occupies an essential position in their life and the degree to which the interests of the child take priority over the interest of the parent (Iwaniec, Herbert & Sluckin, 2002). In order for bonding to be effective, a parent has to be able to 'read' their baby's cues, for example, if they initiate an activity when the child is sleepy, the baby is unlikely to respond in a manner that is reinforcing for parental bonding. Bonding refers to the interactional behaviour of the parent and how they adjust and adapt to match their child's rate of development. In behaviour analysis, bonding is analysed with regard to the effectiveness of reinforcement functions of child responses to parental caregiving behaviours (Dillenburger, 2000). This will be explored further in the next chapter.

*Information processing* theorists focus on individual cognitive processing and suggest that parents:

- Do not perceive the child's signal.
- Interpret the infant's signal as not requiring a response.
- Recognise the signal but are unable to respond.
- Know how to respond appropriately yet do not respond.

They differentiate between disorganised, emotional, and depressed neglect in families who are either crisis-ridden or with inconsistent parenting, who could provide materially for their children but fail to connect emotionally, or who are withdrawn and do not seem motivated to care for their children. Neglectful parents are thought to be unable to process the information necessary for adequate child care and consequently information processing theorists suggest that parent education would be ineffective for this group of parents. Placing the rationale for parenting behaviour within an internal information processing paradigm falls prey to mentalistic reasoning and thus, not surprisingly, it

has been difficult to translate this theory into effective practice.

A broader *socio-ecological framework* focuses on the interaction between a range of variables beyond those of the individual and the family and includes the community and the culture. Neglect is viewed as the result of the interaction of protective and risk factors within these four systems. Similar to the UN Convention for the Rights of the Child, the focus of a socio-economic model is on a child's unmet needs, rather than deficiencies in parents' behaviour. Figure 1.1 shows the wide range of risk and protective factors that are considered within a social-ecological model.

While critics argue that individual parental responsibility is diminished in a social-ecological model, the model includes factors that impact on parenting and thus recognises that while in some extreme cases neglect may be deliberate and malicious, in the majority of cases this is not so.

## Individual and family factors

Most children who grow up in adverse circumstances are not neglected but the risk increases with a number of conditions, including:

- *Parent related aspects*, such as lone parent families, parents with mental health problems or intellectual disabilities, or parents who grew up in the care system.
- *Child related factors*, such as being very young,

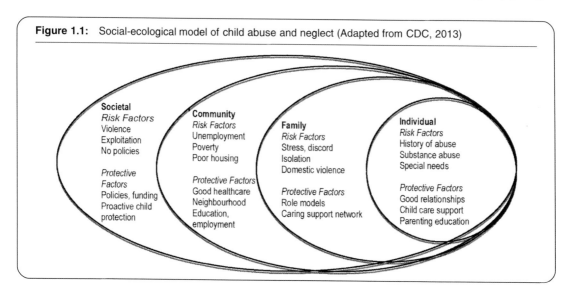

**Figure 1.1:** Social-ecological model of child abuse and neglect (Adapted from CDC, 2013)

**Societal**
*Risk Factors*
Violence
Exploitation
No policies

*Protective Factors*
Policies, funding
Proactive child protection

**Community**
*Risk Factors*
Unemployment
Poverty
Poor housing

*Protective Factors*
Good healthcare
Neighbourhood
Education, employment

**Family**
*Risk Factors*
Stress, discord
Isolation
Domestic violence

*Protective Factors*
Role models
Caring support network

**Individual**
*Risk Factors*
History of abuse
Substance abuse
Special needs

*Protective Factors*
Good relationships
Child care support
Parenting education

having a low birth weight, or being born prematurity.

- *Social economic circumstances*, such as poverty and social isolation.

(Radford, et al. 2011)

Referrals to social care or health services are most likely to involve lone parent families and, given that the main caregivers in most of these families are women, child protection investigations can fall prey to gender stereotyping. Viewing mothers as the main adult responsible for safeguarding the child can lead to neglecting the role of men, in relation to both protective and risk factors (Daniel & Taylor, 2006). Clearly, even absent fathers can pose a risk as well as offering protection from neglect. Equally, new partners that join a lone parent family can have a protective influence that can help stabilise vulnerable families. However, the risk to children increases with the introduction of new unstable or violent partners, especially since new relationships like these are often relatively short-lived and may successively introduce new, unfamiliar, and potentially unsafe adults into the child's life. In some of these cases, child protection services place children on the child protection registers because of concern about risk, isolation, or lack of social support rather than actual harm to or proven neglect of the child.

Given these potential stressors, it is not surprising that lone mothers experience higher risk of mental illness than fathers in similar situations. Parental mental illness has the potential to affect children in many ways, including emotional unavailability of the parent or generally disorganised living conditions and lack of stability. In addition, the child may become a young caregiver for a parent with mental health problems and safeguarding these children can be a delicate issue, especially when the parent genuinely cares about the child, but requires significant levels of care themselves. Parents who misuse drugs or alcohol may not be able to supervise or attend to the safety of the child appropriately and children may be exposed to lack of supervision, inappropriate adult behaviour, or unsafe storage of drugs, needles, or alcohol.

Most parents who have intellectual disabilities can care for their own children given the right support, however, they may well come under closer scrutiny by child protection agencies because of an increased risk of developmental delay for children and if they are already known to social services before the birth of the child. Parents with intellectual disabilities are likely to experience the same life stresses as all parents, but usually have lower levels of formal education, supports, and resources and higher levels of unemployment and poverty and thus often experience poorer living conditions (Feldman, 2004). In particular, those who come to the attention of child protection agencies are likely to have few family supports, lack stability in family circumstances and normal childhood experiences and may have difficult relationships with professionals.

Young women who grew up in care are three times more likely than other young women to become teenage parents. A high number of teenage mothers are lone parents as many teenage fathers are absent and not involved in child care. As children, these mothers may well have experienced frequent changes in caregivers, poor parenting models, interrupted education and consequently be at increased risk of poor outcomes, such as homelessness or problems with addictions. In addition of course, given that they have had long-term involvement with social services, they are more likely to be monitored and such close attention from the child protection system is likely to increase stress and pressure on parents who are already facing difficulties (O'Hagan & Dillenburger, 1995).

Child-related factors that increase vulnerability include prematurity and low birth weight, health problems, and developmental difficulties and disability, or being unwanted. Age and gender of the child are also linked to vulnerability, for example the risk of neglect is particularly pronounced during the first year of life and boys are somewhat more at risk of both physical abuse and neglect (Sidebotham & Heron, 2003). Protective factors that increase resilience include having an easy temperament, being a girl, being attractive to others, having warm supportive parents, good quality housing, adequate financial resources and support from extended family or a close relationship with a trusted adult.

## Community and societal factors

Social support is important for all families, especially for those with young children. Social isolation of parents or caregivers can be a contributory factor in child neglect. The reasons for lack of social support can be diverse; some people may find social contact aversive while others have a lack of social skills or experience stress and other difficulties. Equally, those who could potentially offer social support may avoid parents who are perceived as inadequate or neglectful. Particularly vulnerable parents sometimes place very high demands on peers or family members and may be dissatisfied even when relatively good support is available. Thus, actual as well as perceived lack of sufficient support can lead to social isolation.

Although a correlation between poverty and neglect exists, poverty does not cause neglect. Rather than a single variable poverty is a combination of circumstances not only related to material resources but also to housing, living and working environment, status and power, education, health services and access to leisure. Poverty can be extreme or relative. In developing countries, more than 30% of children (about 600 million) live in extreme poverty (less than US$1 a day) and these children are the first priority of worldwide Millennium development goals (UNICEF, 2013).

Remarkably however, in so-called developed countries the figures of children in relative poverty, in other words with household earnings of less than 60% of the average monthly income, are similar; for example, in the UK, 27% (3.6 million) and in the United States 21% (nearly 15 million) children live in relative poverty; in Belfast relative poverty affects 47% of all children (DoH, 2003). These children experience being hungry, cold, and not being able to go on holidays or join their friends' activities. They tend to be premature at birth, have a low birth weight, achieve less well at school, and suffer more ill health. All of these factors impact on their health and education, as well as their emotional wellbeing and potential to live happy, healthy, productive lives as adults. Of course, neglect is not restricted to children living in poverty, but financial hardship impacts on parents' ability to provide adequate food, shelter, and stimulation for their children and may also cause chronic stress. In fact, families unable to provide for even the most basic needs of children are considered as suffering from societal neglect. As one Glaswegian mother stated 'cause I do not have safety equipment for my child does not mean that I need to be educated in the fact that such equipment exists . . . I simply do not have the money to purchase it' (Rice et al., 1994: 7).

A social-ecological model is useful for exploring possible causes of neglect and for guiding policy-makers at community and society level, while at individual and family levels it can guide direct intervention with individual families that are most difficult to reach and who are most in need of services.

## Summary

Neglect has not been given the same attention as other forms of child abuse. This is because it is difficult to define, due to the long-term cumulative nature of the problem and also because it is difficult to assess because neglect is based on acts of omission, rather than commission (McDaniel & Dillenburger, 2007).

The range of factors that indicate which families are most vulnerable include environmental and personal stresses, such as poverty, social isolation, poor communication skills, relationship problems, poor living conditions, and poor employment prospects. These stressors are more likely to occur among young lone parents or parents with intellectual disabilities and therefore parenting assessments need to take into account the context in which families live.

Whether responsibility for child care is placed entirely within the family or the impact of the wider environment is acknowledged, variations in the definitions and causation models of neglect show how different societies, communities, and individual child care professionals interpret neglect in different ways.

Clearer definitions and better theoretical frameworks are necessary to identify thresholds for parenting standard. An evidence base for effective interventions is needed to allow resources to be spent more efficiently. While medical and psychodynamic approaches are based on an individual disease and pathology model, social-ecological theories view neglect in the context of wider environmental factors. A more holistic approach is needed to understand individual circumstances within a cultural and societal context.

# CHAPTER 2

# Behaviour Analysis

Behaviour analysis is the *natural science* that uses empirical methods to discover behavioural principles. Behaviour is the 'unit of analysis', defined as the interaction of a biological 'organism' with their environment. The main focus is on how environmental changes affect behaviour, although of course, the effects of biological changes on the interaction are also considered (Keenan & Dillenburger, 2012). The utilisation of these discoveries, in other words, the application of this science for the enhancement of socially relevant behaviours is aptly called *Applied Behaviour Analysis* (Cooper et al., 2007). In this chapter, Applied Behaviour Analysis (ABA) is described and examples are given of how ABA is used in a number of areas.

By avoiding mentalistic pseudo-explanations and circular reasoning, behaviour analysis broadens the understanding of child neglect and offers direct immediate guidance for intervention. Behaviour analysis considers individual learning histories, present circumstances and cultural contexts as the key to understanding human behaviour. Thus, it offers precise contextual contingency analyses of functional relationships between individuals and their social and cultural contexts.

Applied behaviour analysis enriches socio-ecological and rights-based perspectives with the rigor of evidence-based practice grounded in a detailed knowledge base of actual behavioural principles. The pragmatist view taken by applied behaviour analysis renders the dualist differentiation of mind/body and its inherent speculation on mentalistic causation unnecessary. Behaviour analysis espouses the holistic view of the internal and external world of the individual being subject to the same natural laws, in other words, individual behaviour is the result of the biological organism interacting with environmental, social, and cultural contexts. In fact, behaviour analysts question the utility of a separation of internal vs. external and propose that 'the skin does not separate you from the world, it unites you to it' (Keenan, 1997: 79). This understanding differs significantly from other approaches to child neglect, for example,

psychoanalytic or medical and disease models, which suggest that internal factors are the cause of behaviour, and pathologies are viewed as emanating from within the individual and are labelled accordingly (cf. DSM-5, 2013).

Behaviour analysis exposes problems with mentalistic labelling (Keenan & Dillenburger, 2012). Clearly, a label does not explain why a person behaves in the way they do, in fact, it merely offers a descriptive summary of behavioural topographies. Commonly, reifications of descriptive summary labels are wrongly used as explanatory fictions, for example, if a child hits and bites other children, these behaviours are correctly summarised as 'aggressive' but then this label is incorrectly reified as 'aggression' or grouped under the summary label of 'conduct disorder'. The term 'aggression' then is used to explain the biting and hitting behaviour, in other words, 'he is doing this because of his aggression' or 'he is doing this because of his conduct disorder' (O'Reilly & Dillenburger, 2000).

The behaviour analytic view that behaviour occurs as a result of interaction of the individual with their environment, rather than originating from within the individual, offers fundamental practice guidance. Accounts that seek to explain causes of behaviour with hypothetical dualistic concepts, such as consciousness or mind are rejected and replaced with a focus on scientific explanations based on empirical examinations of actual causes of privately as well as publicly observable behaviours. Privately observable refers to behaviours that are only observable by the self, in other words, cognitions and emotions that occur 'within the skin' while publically observable refers to behaviours that can be observed by more than one, such as body movements and vocal expressions. The behaviour analytic definition includes public and private behaviour under the umbrella term 'behaviour' and hence differs radically from traditional definitions of behaviour that consider only publically observable events.

Moreover, behaviour analysis focuses on the function of behaviour rather than its topography or structure (Dillenburger & Keenan, 1997).

Structural approaches categorise the topography of behaviour, in other words, the way the behaviour 'looks' in terms of physical movement, under predetermined classifications, while functional approaches explore the purpose that behaviour serves for the individual. Functional behaviour assessments reveal, that behaviours that are entirely different in topography may serve a very similar function and require similar interventions, while behaviours with the same or very similar topographies may serve completely different functions and require quite different interventions (Iwata et al., 1994).

## Basic principles of behaviour

Since the early twentieth century behaviour analytic scientists have investigated the interactive relationship between biological organisms and their environment and have discovered a range of behavioural principles that depend on the biology of the organism under investigation and its learning history as well as the present situation within a cultural context.

One of the most basic behavioural principles, *classical conditioning*, was discovered in the early 20th century (Pavlov, 1903). The key discovery was that when a stimulus (unconditioned stimulus) that elicits genetically programmed reflexes is paired with a neutral stimulus (a stimulus that originally does not elicit these reflexes) this can lead to the neutral stimulus becoming a conditioned stimulus. In other words, the previously neutral stimulus elicits the same behaviours or reflexes as the unconditioned stimulus and more importantly, this happens in the absence of the unconditioned stimulus. Classical conditioning generally involves involuntary behaviour and is thought to be a key factor in the development of a range of clinical conditions including anxiety, phobias, and depression. However, classical conditioning occurs in many other day-to-day situations and many of the most common reinforcers are established by classical conditioning (more in a moment).

Classical conditioning is the behavioural principle that is utilised in intervention methodologies such as systematic desensitisation, where first, a relaxation-inducing stimulus is used as unconditioned stimulus and then the fear or anxiety generating stimuli are gradually introduced either in an imagined or in-vivo

stimulus hierarchy until relaxation becomes the conditioned response and replaces the initial fear or anxiety response.

Another fundamental behavioural principle includes the fact that what happens before a behaviour occurs (the antecedent stimulus) is important, but also what happens after the behaviour occurs (the consequent stimulus) can determine the probability of behaviour occurring or reoccurring. Operant conditioning is the term used to describe the discovery of how behaviour affects, in other words, operates on and is affected by the environment, in other words, how antecedent and consequent stimuli influence behaviour (Skinner, 1974). Operant behaviour is *emitted* voluntarily, rather than being elicited as in classical conditioning.

The basic unit in operant conditioning is the *three-term contingency*, in other words, Antecedent, Behaviour and Consequence, also known as the 'ABC'. The future probability of the behaviour is a function of the if-then relationship between these three elements, particularly the consequences of the behaviour. Consequent stimuli that lead to an increase in the future probability of the behaviour are called *reinforcers* and those that lead to a decrease in the future probability of the behaviour are called *punishers*.

*Reinforcers* and *punishers* are defined by the effect that they have on behaviour, not by the intent of the person who is providing the consequence, in other words, something cannot be described as a reinforcer unless it has been shown to *increase* the probability of the behaviour recurring. The same in reverse is true for punishers. A consequence is only a punisher if it has been shown to *decrease* the probability of the behaviour recurring. Given this functional definition of reinforcement and punishment, the range of stimuli that can function as reinforcers and punishers is endless and depends nearly entirely on individual learning histories.

Reinforcers and punishers can be unconditioned or conditioned. Unconditioned reinforcers and punishers have some kind of survival value, for example, food or shelter commonly function as reinforces, increasing the probability of the behaviour that led to access to them. In contrast, the heat of an open flame functions commonly as a punisher, reducing the likelihood of recurrence of behaviour that led to a burn.

Conditioned reinforcers and punishers gain their functional value through association with unconditioned reinforcers or punishers through classical conditioning or through secondary conditioning, in other words, being paired with another conditioned reinforce/punisher. Conditioned reinforcers can include tangible items such as a toy or money or other social stimuli, such as verbal praise, while conditioned punishers can include fines or other social stimuli, such as reprimands. But remember, these stimuli are only reinforcers or punishers if they have the apposite function on the future probability of the behaviour under scrutiny.

Obviously then, given differences in the learning history of individuals something that acts as a reinforcer or punisher for one person's behaviour will not necessarily function in the same way for someone else's. To complicate matters, the same reinforcer or punisher does not work for the same behaviour all of the time. *Motivational operations* (Michael, 1993) such as saturation, deprivation, or other significant experiences can change the effectiveness of a consequence as a reinforcer or punisher. They can either establish a reinforcer such as making a previously weak reinforcer stronger or they can *abolish* a reinforcer, such that a previously strong reinforcer no longer functions very well to strengthen the behaviour under consideration.

In applied settings, if a consequence does not increase the strength of behaviour this does not mean that the principle of reinforcement does not work, instead it means that the reinforcer that could be effective under the given circumstances has not been identified yet. Similarly, if a consequence does not reduce the probability of the behaviour recurring it means that the functionally effective punisher has not been identified (Grant & Evans, 1994). Basically, if we find a behaviour at high frequency, for example if a parent or teacher tells you that 'he always does that' you should be searching to identify the reinforcer at play.

Reinforcers and punishers are classed as positive if a stimulus is added (+) after behaviour has occurred; they are considered negative (−) if a stimulus is deducted or taken away. The terms positive and negative have absolutely nothing to do with any value judgement, they are simply shorthand for a plus + (positive) or minus − (negative) equation. Both positive and negative reinforcement lead to an increase in the probability of behaviour recurring. For the most part, a positive reinforcer is something that is desired while a negative reinforcer increases

behaviour that allows for escape or avoidance of an aversive stimulus, such as a difficult task. But this is not always or necessarily the case. Things that would be considered by most to be aversive can function as positive reinforcers, for example, a smack can lead to increases in crying behaviour. It all depends on the focus of the analysis.

Both positive and negative punishers lead to a decrease in the probability of the behaviour recurring; again, the positive (+) refers to something being added, and the negative (−) refers to something being taken away. Generally (but not necessarily) a positive punisher is aversive, in other words a consequence that is not desired, while a negative punisher is the removal of a desired stimulus, for example, a fine is the removal of money. Of course all of these examples only apply if the consequences have the defined function on the behaviour and are not related to the qualification of a stimulus as either aversive or desired.

Given the many unintended side effects of punishment, for example, it only teaches what not to do rather than teaching what to do (Sidman, 1989) behaviour analysts generally avoid the use of punishment procedures and prefer to focus on reinforcement-based interventions. Initially if nothing else works, some interventions are based on arbitrary or conditioned positive reinforcers, for example, token economies. However in order to generalise and maintain desired intervention effects, arbitrary reinforcers are replaced as soon as possible by reinforcers that occur as a natural consequence of the target behaviour. The planned, scheduled move from arbitrary to natural reinforcers influences the future rate and strength of the behaviour in natural non-clinical settings and is the key to maintaining behaviour change.

There are many methods to achieve behavioural maintenance. Using fixed ratio or fixed interval *schedules of reinforcement* means that the behaviour is reinforced every time the exact ratio (number of responses) or interval (time lapse) has been achieved. Fixed reinforcement schedules are useful and often necessary to establish new behaviours but can lead to fairly rigid patterns of behaviour with a *post reinforcement pause* (low performance) after each reinforce delivery. In contrast, variable ratio and variable interval schedules, where the number of responses (ratio) or time lapse (interval) are not fixed and thus reinforcers are delivered intermittently, lead to steady, strong performances with no post reinforcement pauses, and are as such much more useful when the maintenance of behavioural gains is the target.

Although behavioural interventions often focus on adjusting consequences to achieve the target behaviour, much can be achieved through attention to the *antecedents*. Many antecedent stimuli are already conditioned through an individual's learning histories and as such set the contexts in which specific behaviours occur. Temporally distal antecedents such as *setting events* can influence the effects of proximal contingencies; for example, if a young parent, who usually competently engages in child care tasks, got into a fight with her partner in the morning, she could miss out on feeding her baby at lunchtime, but if she settled down again by the afternoon, she could competently feed her baby at dinner time. Consequently, people behave differently in different contexts and settings and the skilful use of stimulus discrimination and control in therapy and education can prevent the need for more complex contingency management in many situations.

Modelling and observational learning are important ways to attain new behaviours using antecedent/stimulus control. The behaviour of the model becomes a discriminative stimulus for the observer's imitation response, especially if the model's behaviour is positively reinforced, in other words, through vicarious reinforcement. Modelling can be used to teach new behaviour, including communication, self-care skills, and better performance from employees, often with more rapid results than contingency shaping procedures (Grant & Evans, 1994). Of course, some unwanted behaviour may also be learned, for example, parents who use physical punishment to stop children from fighting or using violence are modelling the very behaviour they are trying to prevent.

The behaviour of the model is more likely to be imitated if it is reinforced, the imitator has generalised imitation skills, and the model shows positive attitudes and emotions and is:

- Successful at the task.
- Perceived to be high status, for example, a child who is popular in class.
- Similar to the observer.
- Consistent in their performance.

Modelling and imitation occur frequently in the natural environment and are utilised in many therapy settings (Lindsay et al., 2013). An infant's imitative behaviour is often heavily reinforced by parents, for example, in playing games such as 'peek a boo'. These kinds of games allow children to develop generalised imitation skills.

Rules also are very powerful antecedents that govern much of human behaviour. Rule-governed behaviour differs from contingency shaped behaviour in that it is based on a description of a contingency, rather than on direct contact with contingencies. A rule gains stimulus control over the behaviour of language able humans because it specifies the contingencies that operate in a certain situation (Skinner, 1966). Of course, the behaviour of adhering to rules has to be learned and generalised. Generally speaking there is a qualitative difference between learning by rules, such as reading and being told to do something or learning by doing. Learning by doing means that behaviour of the learner can be directly reinforced and thus shaped to the level of mastery (Keenan & Dillenburger, 2000).

*Generalisation* is achieved when newly learned behaviour, such as 'following a particular rule' or 'imitating a certain model', is evoked by a variety of stimuli, settings, or people outside training conditions and becomes a general ability for example, to 'follow a variety of rules and instructions' or 'imitate a numerous models and behaviours'. *Maintenance* is achieved when behaviour changes endure in the long-term, in other words, when the behaviour and skills that have been learned and established during intervention, are still in place in a month, a year or 5 years later. It is not enough to hope that behaviour change is generalised and maintained. Generalisation and maintenance are accomplished by including as many other people as possible, for example, peers and other significant people in the intervention and using them as models and to reinforce new behaviours. It is also achieved by fading arbitrary reinforcers and replacing them with naturally occurring reinforcers, the use of intermittent schedules of reinforcement, and occasional reinforcement of generalised behaviour (cf. Cooper et al., 2007). Without a doubt, generalisation and maintenance of intervention goals are of central importance in working with parents and caregivers in child neglect.

## Research methodology

As a scientific discipline behaviour analysis requires specificity and precision. The main research methodology in behaviour analysis is the

Single System Design [SSD]. In SSD, the target behaviour is very clearly defined and measured along one or more specific dimensions, for example, frequency, duration, latency, or inter-response time, to establish a baseline prior to the intervention being put in place. Continuous measurements during and after intervention evidence the effectiveness of the intervention. Hence, SSD uses intra-subject comparison rather than statistical analysis of inter-group averages to achieve internal validity. External validity is achieved through replication (Johnston & Pennypacker, 1993).

Commonly used SSD are

1.  ABAB reversal design with follow-up, where A depicts the baseline, B the intervention phase. The return to baseline is used to ensure that effects observed during B are truly due to the intervention and nothing else, before re-introducing the intervention and collecting follow-up data.
2.  Multiple baseline designs across behaviours, situations, or participants, where a number of different baselines are taken and interventions are sequentially introduced, while baselines are continued on the comparator parameters, thus evidencing and achieving experimental control.
3.  Changing criterion designs that start with relatively easily achievable criteria and once this is achieved the criterion is increased progressively until the target behaviour is achieved.
4.  Alternating treatment designs that ensure experimental control through randomly alternating conditions, to evidence the superior effect of one intervention over the others.

Examples and more details about these designs are provided in Chapter 5.

A science that demands this level of precision and specificity requires clear definitions. Therefore questions in behaviour analysis are couched in 'SMART' terms to ensure they are specific, measurable, attainable, realistic, and timely.

- *Specific* means that 'W' questions must be answered: *Who* is involved? *What* is to be achieved? *Where* (location) is it happening? *When* (time frame) is it happening? *How* (exact description of behaviour) is it happening? In other words, a detailed definition of the behaviour is necessary.
- *Measurable* means that concrete criteria for measuring must be established. These include behavioural dimensions, such as measuring the behavioural frequency, duration, latency, intensity, and inter-response time.
- *Attainable*, Realistic and Timely include the requirements that targets are socially valid. Social validity procedures include measures on relevance, importance, acceptability, meaningfulness, and appropriateness of intervention goal, intervention, and outcome.

## Summary

Conventionally, explanations of behaviour are based on inferences drawn from descriptive labels. Attributing a person's behaviour to internal events, cognitions, or individual personality traits gives the appearance of an explanation. Skinner (1974: 175) recognised that 'many supposed inner causes of behaviour, such as attitudes, opinions, traits of character, and philosophies, remain almost entirely inferential'. Inferential explanations are hypothetical, based on reification and circular reasoning but tend to give the appearance of having achieved an explanation, in other words, they are explanatory fiction (Keenan & Dillenburger, 2012). Consequently full explorations of environmental, historic, and genetic setting events, motivation operations, and antecedents or consequences of behaviour are not conducted. Behavioural explanations of neglect explore genetic, historic, and environmental influences on current behaviour using behavioural principles, rather than relying on inferential pseudo-explanations.

# CHAPTER 3

# Behaviour Analysis and Child Neglect

Although problems in interaction between parent and child are often seen as central to exploring the aetiology of abuse and neglect (Iwaniec, 2004) directly neglectful or abusive behaviours are unlikely to be observed by professionals. Parents are unlikely to maltreat their children in the presence of an observer because of the professional obligation to report such action. However, observing other day-to-day interactions makes it possible to obtain a picture of how the family interacts, and establish the common antecedents and consequences of negative interactions. This is based on the assumption that neglectful or abusive acts are part of a continuum of everyday behaviours within a family and are learned and maintained and thus subject to the same behavioural principles as other behaviours that would not be classed as abuse or neglect. In this chapter, child neglect is examined from a behaviour analytic perspective.

SMART conditions are difficult to achieve in terms of neglect, given that while *abuse* is related to the commission, or excess, of problematic parental behaviours towards the child, *neglect* relates to the omission, or lack, of adequately caring parenting behaviours (CDC, 2013). Additionally, neglect is not usually the outcome of one incident; the effects are cumulative and build up over time. Moreover, the range of behaviours that result in child neglect may not be directly related to child care. An example is parental substance misuse that may lead to a child being neglected, injured, or harmed because of lack of supervision (Mattaini & Thyer, 1996). This makes neglectful caregiver behaviours difficult to define and explain.

In behaviour analysis the term *neglect* is considered a descriptive summary label of behaviours or behavioural outcomes. On one level the term sums up the behaviours of those responsible for the care of the child, be they parents, other caregivers, or society as a whole; on another level, the term describes behavioural outcomes for the child: the child is neglected, in other words, his or her needs are not adequately met and 'it shows'. The term itself does not explain anything nor does it identify desired caregiver behaviours or desired child related outcomes. The term merely sums up a range of behaviours with a descriptive label.

Faced with a descriptive summary label, the first thing a behaviour analyst does is to ask for a concrete behavioural definition, a list of behaviours that fall under the umbrella of the descriptive summary label. Given the lack of internationally agreed child care standards, it is impossible to list the kinds of caregiver behaviours that would fall under the summary label *neglect*. With regard to child outcomes, the United Nations Convention on the Rights of the Child (CRC) described in Chapter 1 gives some indication of internationally agreed standards or outcomes for children, for example, the right to safety, food, shelter, education, play etc., but these are not specified in precise, or measurable terms.

The CRC does not set out precise desired caregiver behaviours, although it sets out a general framework that mandates Governmental support for caregivers who struggle to achieve the general goals for children's rights. The CRC also includes a monitoring system for governments who fail to achieve these goals. Therefore, it might be useful to assume that a child is neglected if their rights under the CRC are not met; but since the CRC categories are not very concrete or individually tailored, this still remains open to interpretation.

## Functional assessment

Behavioural work begins with the collection of assessment or baseline data using a range of methods including direct observations or service user self-reports to generate a *functional assessment* of the contingencies that maintain, restrict or reduce child care behaviour. The functions of behaviour, once established, form the basis of intervention design.

Assessing contingencies of which omission of adequate child care behaviour is a function begins with a close look at proximal and distal antecedents. *Proximal* or current antecedents immediately precipitate neglect, for example, a caregiver drinking heavily during the day, leaving them unable to provide adequate meals for their children or a phone call with a friend that takes precedence over attending a crying baby. *Distal* or *historical antecedents* are events that happen some time before the neglect but are associated with it directly or indirectly, for example, a caregiver's experience of neglect in their own childhood may directly leave them insufficiently skilled in caregiving behaviours while unemployment causes stress that could indirectly impact on a caregiver's ability to provide adequate educational support for a child.

*Structural antecedents* are aspects of the person's environment that are relatively permanent, such as lasting environmental stresses, poverty, crowded living conditions, marital conflict, lack of resources, low educational achievement, or physical or psychological limitations of caregiver. Public policy interventions are likely to address structural antecedents, for example, anti-poverty strategies and the provision of good quality public housing or safe play areas. It can be difficult to trace these kinds of antecedents accurately because they may be part of a complex chain of events that have impacted on caregiver behaviour over time.

*Discriminative stimuli* and contextual cues are conditioned antecedents that have come to signal whether behaviour is likely to be reinforced or not. For child care tasks, the stimulus can be the time of day, for example, for meal times, indicating that sitting at the table will lead to being fed or the time of year, for example, winter, signifying that wearing skimpy clothes will be punished by being cold. Cues from the child can also act as discriminatory stimuli or cues for caring behaviour, for example, when a baby cries this may indicate that they are hungry and that feeding them will stop the crying. When naturally occurring cues do not act as an antecedent for caretaking behaviours, more artificial prompts are needed, for example written or pictorial signs, verbal cues, or having set times of day to carry out tasks.

*Motivating operations* (MO) alter the effectiveness of reinforcing or punishing consequences, thereby modifying the probability of the occurrence of contingent behaviour. With regard to child neglect this means that 'operations', such as social isolation, can alter the effectiveness of a consequence that in the past functioned as reinforcers for child care behaviours. For example, when a socially isolated parent is offered social contact, such as a friend asking them to go to the cinema, the movie-going behaviour is likely to take precedence over child care behaviours even if they were usually carried out appropriately. To complicate matters, a specific MO can affect a range of different behaviours, while a particular behaviour could be affected by a number of MOs.

*Rules* and verbal instructions differ from other antecedents because they alter behaviour by describing contingencies, rather than through actual contingency exposure. Rule-governed behaviour is important because it allows behaviour to be learned quickly and efficiently and is necessary for many elements of child care, particularly those that do not have obvious or immediate consequences, such as medical guidelines leading parents to bringing a child to the doctor or learning to feed their child a healthy diet. The immediate effects of these behaviours may not necessarily function as a reinforcer, in fact the child may protest when given a vaccination or presented with healthy food. The reinforcement provided by the child's good health is likely to be a delayed consequence and has to be included in the instruction explicitly. Of course in the short-term, an encouraging comment can function to bridge the time gap and reinforce a parent's caretaking behaviour.

Adherence to rules will depend on the individual's learning history with regard to following rules and instructions. Child care repertoires are generally only reinforced if they are socially accepted, adhere to the social conventions of the extended family, and follow the norms and values of a culture or community. Parents who have been neglected or maltreated as children sometimes develop their own, possibly misguided, child care rules and failure to comply with community cultural rules relating to child care practice can result in these parents being ostracised and isolated.

Guiding behaviour with appropriate rules is also important when contingencies are dangerous to test out, for example, leaving a young child alone in the bath or allowing a young child to cross the road without supervision. In these circumstances it is clearly safer if the parent has learned the rule, 'Do not to leave a child unsupervised', rather than learning this through trial and error. Parents who have difficulties with providing adequate child care may not have received suitable reinforcement for parenting behaviours and difficulties are increased if they do not have a history of reinforcement for following rules within the social environment.

Nonetheless, there are drawbacks to the over-use of rules and instructions in parent training, especially if the contingencies specified in the rules are not immediately tested and therefore 'adherence to the rule' is not reinforced. Also, over-compliance to instruction may lead to parenting practices that are not sensitive to the child's individual momentary needs and therefore can become neglectful, for example, a parent who has a fixed routine for child care tasks such as feeding may not adapt the routine, even if the child is unwell and needs more but smaller meals. This means that even parenting behaviours that were learned initially through a rule or instruction require practical experience; in behaviour analytic terms 'direct exposure to contingencies', so as to become responsive to contextual cues and cues from the child.

*Modelling or observational learning* are important processes for explaining existing and acquiring new behaviours. Observational learning is a form of operant behaviour although the reinforcers may not be obvious. Imitation skills are shaped in early childhood through peek-a-boo and other similar games. However, not every child learns imitations skills easily, for example, many children on the autistic spectrum need to be taught explicitly how to imitate and procedures need to be put in place to ensure imitation becomes a generalised skill for these children (Lindsay et al., 2013).

Furthermore, the opportunity to observe a model does not guarantee that the observer will perform, in other words, imitate the behaviour, they need the component skills to carry out the new behaviour. This means that people cannot learn really advanced parenting skills through imitation before learning more basic foundation skills.

Observational learning is an important source for learning parenting behaviour and like rule-governed behaviour allows parents to learn behaviours without experiencing immediate consequences. Many basic child care skills are learned through imitation of a model who is competent in the skills. Most of us learn how to look after a baby or child from models who are available within the family, socially, or in the media. Parents who are socially isolated and live in environments where neglectful child care is accepted as the norm, or have been maltreated themselves in their childhood may lack appropriate role models and subsequently have difficulties with parenting behaviours when they become parents themselves, simply because they have never experienced apposite parenting models. Modelling appropriate parenting behaviours, for example, through group work or video modelling, can be a very effective intervention in these cases.

## Child related issues

Given that the majority of *distal* and *proximal* consequences for appropriate parenting behaviour are provided by the child's response, it is important to consider child behaviours and characteristics and their impact on parenting behaviour. Children are active participants in the interaction with parents and others in their lives. Of course, this is not to suggest that children are in any way responsible for maltreatment, but it is the case that some children are more difficult to care for than others and that these children are more at risk of neglect. Characteristics that leave a child vulnerable to abuse or neglect include a child being very young, <5 years of age; being 'colicky' or 'cranky' with prolonged episodes of crying; or if the child has a disability. Of course, these factors in themselves do not affect the standard of care a child receives, much more depends on parents' skills and social supports, but they do play a part in the overall vulnerability because they are likely to increase stress levels to which young parents are exposed.

Before birth a child can be exposed to a range of factors that can impact on subsequent development, these include nutrition, toxins, medication, drugs, alcohol, maternal activity, and parental age. These factors influence risk or protective factors for the development of the foetal nervous system and consequently impact on activity level, emotional responsiveness, mood quality, and social adaptability, responses commonly summarised under the term 'temperament'.

Temperament tests identify the behavioural capacity of an infant to attend, differentiate and habituate to a range of stimuli. These stimuli include touch, rocking, and facial expressions that are used to soothe or alert the infant. Measures are taken of vigour, motor activity, muscle tone, and colour changes as the infant's state of arousal changes.

Individual temperaments are categorised as *easy*, *difficult*, or *slow to warm up* and linked to vulnerability to abuse or neglect (Iwaniec, 2004). Children who are assessed as having an 'easy' temperament are thought to provide more reinforcers for caregiver behaviour and are thus considered easier to care for because of their regular reactions, positive mood, and adaptability to new situations. Children with a so-called 'difficult' temperament provide more aversive consequences for caregiver behaviour and thus are considered more difficult to care for. 'Slow to warm up' children are slow to adapt to or withdraw from new situations thus providing inconsistent consequences for caregiver behaviour.

Temperament is thought to be a combination of genetic and environmental influences, with genetic influences becoming less pertinent as exposure to environmental factors increases. The influence of environment on temperament is a two-way process. While a child's early responses to their environment influences the response of the caregivers to the child, clearly 'temperament' is also shaped by experience and may change over time. A child classified as having an easy temperament, may be very quiet and content and therefore more easily ignored by a parent than an active child. In extreme cases, this could lead to neglect of the 'easy' child especially if parents are distracted by other stresses in their life. Consequently the child could become difficult, withdrawn or passive due to lack of contingent attention. On the other hand, the same child receiving ample caregiver attention and stimulation could remain 'easy', happily active, and engaged.

The child's relationship with the parent is commonly described as attachment. For the behaviour analyst the term *attachment* is considered a summary label, a metaphor for a range of specific child behaviours concerned with the child's relationship to their parents that are influenced by many circumstances and contingencies. Like any other behaviours these relationships are considered subject to the laws of behaviour. The idea of an internal working model of attachment, discussed in Chapter 1, is considered hypothetical and untestable and is likely to hinder the exploration of wider environmental causes of behaviour (Schlinger, 1995). If a child's specific behaviour is labelled as evidencing attachment, professionals may not look beyond this inferred internal entity, in other words, fall prey to circular reasoning as follows: They observe the child crying when the caregiver

leaves and label this 'attachment' and in turn they then say that the behaviour is caused by attachment, for example, 'He is doing this because he has . . . attachment'.

The real reason for the child's behaviour can be found in early experiences and interaction with the environment that includes, of course, caregiver responses to the baby's behaviour:

> *From birth onwards, infants and those around them, primarily the parents, engage in increasingly complex social interactions in which the behavior of the parents affects the behavior of infants and vice versa, and the behaviors of both are changed as a result.*
>
> (Schlinger, 1995: 185)

The most important social interactions that can be grouped together under the descriptive summary label of 'attachment' are cuddling, signalling, smiling, approach, and crying. These behaviours become increasingly more responsive to specific social stimuli associated with the caregiver. When an infant's protests, such as crying at separation from the parent has the function on the parent's response of delaying or shortening separation, the baby's behaviour is likely to be repeated.

Testing attachment through experiments such as the 'Strange Situation' may overlook the mother's behaviour in past situations and it does not account for the context in which the child has learned these behaviours. A child is likely to behave in different ways in different settings. Mothers who deliberately shape non-protest responses in their child on separation could be 'blamed' for poor attachment of their children. Clearly, a child's reaction to separation from a caregiver is linked to immediate and long-term contingencies and variations in infant behaviour need to be explained through the child's individual learning history with the parent.

Without doubt, infant behaviours are shaped by the parental responses. Initially for the new-born baby, crying is a reflexive behaviour that soon becomes amenable to reinforcers provided by parental responses. When a tired baby cries, inexperienced parents tend to try all sorts of methods to soothe the crying infant, maybe even over-stimulating the baby with attention, music, lifting them up, and thus inadvertently, crying may be reinforced, in other words, crying may increase in frequency, duration, or intensity. When the baby is settled and quietly plays, making happy vocalisations, or entertaining herself, less experienced parents may give little attention and thus inadvertently withhold reinforcement for relaxed behaviour, with the potential result that settled behaviour might extinguish. In this example, the baby learns that crying, rather than making happy 'goo-goo gaa-gaa' vocalisations, is the main cue for getting parental attention. Accordingly, the infant's crying is positively reinforced by parental attention – and increases. More experienced parents may give more attention to settled behaviour and use a quieter less reinforcing approach to try and get the crying baby to sleep, thus teaching the baby early on to self-soothe. Infants unable to self-regulate often experience a range of difficulties later on, including sleep disorders, feeding problems, temper tantrums and hyperactivity.

Generally speaking, young children are likely to behave in ways that provide predictable responses (Schlinger, 1995). In other words, children tend to respond in ways that shape parental behaviour, making it more predictable, even if it is adverse. When parents occasionally or intermittently respond to their child's signals, they are likely to strengthen signalling behaviour. This can lead to problems in parent-child interaction if the behaviour that is reinforced makes increasing demands on a parent who is already very stressed and withdrawn from the child. In contrast, when parents consistently fail to respond to a child's cues, the child is likely to initially become unsettled and more demanding (in behavioural terms this would be considered an extinction burst) before finally stopping the signalling to parents. As the infant's interaction with the world becomes more complex and wider environmental influences function to shape their behaviour, the baby's responses continue to shape parental behaviours and vice versa.

## Parent related issues

There are of course many influences on parent behaviour, most of which were discussed in Chapter 1. Here we will focus on the aetiology of actual parenting behaviours. As we learned earlier, consequences are events or conditions that follow behaviour and increase or decrease the likelihood that the behaviour will reoccur. Long-term exposure to stress, unemployment, drug use etc. are distal antecedent and/or 'setting events' that may reduce the value of reinforcers, including those provided by the child's responses to care giving behaviours. Clearly, 'a parent who

is deprived of important reinforcers and pressed by multiple aversives is less likely to act in care taking and nurturing ways and is more likely to act aggressively toward or ignore the child' (Mattaini & Thyer, 1996: 244).

Consequences for adequate child care practices are proximal or distal. An example of immediate reinforcement is a child who smiles when approached by his mother. If the child's smile positively reinforces the mother's approach behaviour it increases the probability that the mother's behaviour will be repeated. Behaviour is strengthened by immediate delivery of reinforcers.

However, if reinforcers are delayed or distal, especially during the early phase of learning, behaviour is less likely to be repeated, for example, if the regular feeding of an infant is only reinforced by the infant's weight gain or other long-term health benefits, the delay between the two events may be too long to function directly on parenting behaviours. In this case, it may be necessary to identify reinforcers earlier in the chain of behaviour in order to establish feeding behaviour. Another problem with delayed reinforcers is that other behaviours will occur in the time between emission of target response and delivery of reinforcer and therefore these other, possibly undesired, behaviours may be reinforced and increase.

The absence of reinforcing consequences for appropriate child care behaviour can maintain neglecting or maltreating parental behaviours. If the child's wellbeing does not function as a reinforcer for parental care-taking behaviour external or arbitrary reinforcers may have to be put in place, such as praise from family, friends, or professionals or token systems. Equally, when the family is socially isolated and social supports in the community are not available they do not have access to reinforcers for positive child care behaviours; in fact alternative or neglectful behaviours may be reinforced.

Parenting behaviour, like any other behaviour, is a function of contextual contingencies. If it is not reinforced, the frequency and quality of interaction will decrease. Lack of reinforcement for parenting behaviour can lead to the development of distancing, neglect, and depression. Of course, the reverse can also be true; parents who suffer from depression for other reasons may not be able to reinforce child attachment behaviours adequately and sensitively. Children are thought to be most susceptible to the effects of parental depression between six and eighteen months, although the direct impact of depression is difficult to differentiate from other stresses in the parent's life.

Since depression is more often diagnosed for women, more is known about the effects of maternal depression. However, this does not mean that depression does not affect fathers and their relationship with the child. Postnatal depression is thought to affect 10–12% of all mothers and is likely to have a negative impact on children's cognitive development. Due to generally low levels of social support, adolescent mothers are at increased risk of postnatal depression. Depression decreases the sensitivity to social reinforcers and depressed mothers are therefore likely to engage in lower rates of positive exchanges and may be less sensitive to their infants' social cues. Infants are likely to imitate emotional behaviours they observe and may become withdrawn and discontented when interacting with their mothers or other adults. Delays in children's cognitive, social, and emotional development can be difficult to overcome even when postnatal depression is no longer an issue for the parent.

Social isolation can be a consequence of neglect as well as an antecedent. It is just one of many interlinked stresses that can impact on parenting. Social contact and support is a complex issue, it is clearly not just the quantity of contact that counts. Interestingly, families who have come to the attention of child safeguarding services, often live quite close to the grandparental generation or siblings and friends, but generally have difficult and conflicted relationships with them because they either lack the skills or opportunities to avail of these networks or even view social contact as aversive. Parents who have many external stresses and sparse social support networks are at increased risk of interpersonal problems outside their families and may not be able to give their child adequate attention.

## Summary

Child care behaviours are learned through the same basic behavioural principles and processes as other behaviours and are subject to a wide range of influences; what serves as antecedent for one behaviour for one person may not function in the same way for others. Equally, stimuli that function as reinforcers for one behaviour at one time for one person may not function in the same way for another behaviour, at another time, for another person. Another phenomenon is the fact that something that functions as an antecedent stimulus in one situation, may function as a reinforcing stimulus in another situation.

In brief, behaviour occurs within continuous 'streams', constantly changing. In addition, each individual behavioural stream interfaces with the behavioural streams and patterns of others (Keenan & Dillenburger, 2012). In order to parent successfully, parents must have access to the basics like food and housing and need to be able to imitate adequate child care models and follow complex rules as well as having environmental supports that reinforce appropriate child care behaviours. If parents do not have these resources and consequently are not gaining these skills, they are likely to encounter complications that are reflected in child care.

Child abuse or neglect does not occur as the result of a single factor or characteristic of the parent or the child. It evolves because of the interplay of individual, family and social factors. Direct observation of parent-child interaction can give a picture of how the parent and child influence each other's behaviour. As with other areas of parenting, a parent's past experience and current stressors or supports impact on their ability to interact with their child (Iwaniec, 2006).

# CHAPTER 4

# Behavioural Parent Education

Behavioural parent education is recommended when parents ask for help with specific child behaviour problems or when a thorough and individualised assessment of parent-child interactions indicates a lack of parenting skills that put children at risk of neglect or abuse. This chapter delineates the main issues concerned with behavioural parent education with regard to preventing child neglect.

Parent education or training generally covers a wide range of methods, settings and disciplines. Behavioural parent education is based on knowledge of the scientific discipline of behaviour analysis and aims to enable parents to learn different ways of interacting with their children. Behavioural parent education is offered either to groups of parents or case specifically, to individual parents. Educational methods are based on a collaborative model and include coaching and feedback, video or in-vivo modelling and role-play, instruction, rehearsal, and triadic methods that involve the professional, the parent, and the child.

## The bottom-up approach

There are two broad approaches to parent education best visualised in a pyramid diagram (Figure 4.1). The first one, the *top-down approach*, focuses on teaching specific interventions techniques, for example, token systems or 'time out', rather than teaching the behavioural principles that underpin specific behaviour change methods (more to this later). Parent-training programmes that are based on this approach offer very little or no training in the basics of applied behaviour analysis. Not surprisingly then, parents or professionals who are trained simply in the application of one or two specific behaviour change protocols are not flexible or able to help in cases that lie outside their training.

In the other approach, the *bottom-up approach*, parents are taught the key basic behavioural principles first including the basics of functional contingency analysis outlined in Chapter 2.

Clearly, professionals who engage in bottom-up behavioural parent education must have training in and understanding of the basic principles and functions of behaviour themselves; this includes an assessment of individual, family, societal and cultural contexts outlined in Chapter 1. Once parents have learned about basic behaviour analytic foundations, they can explore different ways of how to apply these individually with their own children, to reinforce appropriate behaviour, reduce unwanted behaviour and maintain pro-social behaviour (see Simple Steps, 2013).

Parents should be involved in all stages of intervention, in other words, deciding and recording the target behaviour, identifying the contingencies that maintain problematic behaviour, and implementing interventions in the home. Involving parents in assessment and intervention helps to recognise the impact parents have on their child's behaviour and development and allows the withdrawal of professional services once parents have developed the necessary skills; it is the foundation of parental empowerment. Parental involvement is also advantageous when working with diverse cultural groups as it ensures that plans for interventions reflect the parents' personal values and goals.

If a family experiences a high rate of external stresses, such as poverty, depression, and lack of social support, or where abuse or neglect are severe and long established, a variety of other supports in addition to behavioural parent education may be necessary. Individual work with parents may be necessary to address issues that impact on their ability to care for their children before parent education is likely to be effective. This may include teaching parents stress management techniques such as relaxation, anger control, or problem solving techniques. Developing parental coping skills offers increased protection for children, particularly when they are combined with behavioural parent education to improve child management skills. Of course, it is important to focus on parenting skills as early as

**Figure 4.1:**   Pyramid approach of behaviour parent education

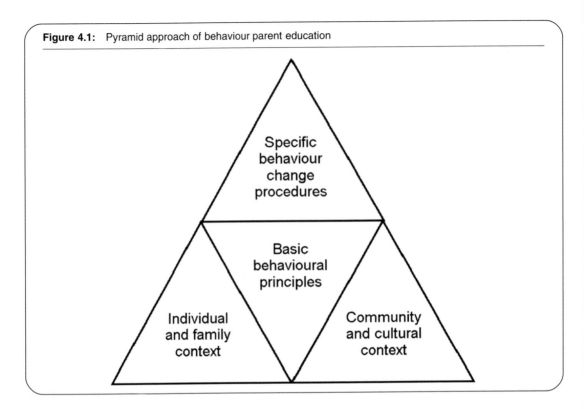

possible when the children are very young, to prevent child problem behaviour from developing.

Evidently, parents who are at greatest risk of maltreating children are also most likely to drop out of parent education programmes. This can be prevented if the programme content is adjusted to parents' needs and the location and timing of sessions are flexible and suitable, when child care is provided for the duration of the sessions, and a collaborative model involves parents in the design of the programme.

## Selecting target behaviours

In behavioural parent education generally a range of behaviours may be targeted, linked directly or indirectly to parenting. In the context of child neglect, the 'omission' aspect is addressed through shaping new child care skills and increasing frequency and duration of existing child care related behaviours. In cases of child maltreatment, the 'commission' aspect is concentrated on through reducing abusive behaviours and building alternative repertoires. Behavioural parent education programmes that focus on difficulties with child behaviours aim to build child management skills.

By-and-large behavioural parent education focuses on ways to increase appropriate behaviours; there are nearly always alternative behaviours that are incompatible or even competing with the undesired response. When it comes to changing child behaviours, parents may need some help initially in identifying alternative or incompatible behaviours. The mantra of a good behavioural parent educator is 'Catch them being good', in other words, parents are guided to focus on desired child behaviours and learn how to improve, establish, and maintain functionally defined target behaviours. Cleary, while the children are being 'good' they are not 'misbehaving'. The main process by which behaviours are established, increased, and maintained is, of course, *reinforcement*. Therefore, 'catch them being good' is convenient shorthand for 'keeping the focus on reinforcement contingencies rather than punishment contingencies'. The effects of behaviour parent education are more likely to be maintained if the emphasis is on skills acquisition and behaviour change and include plans for generalisation so as the ensure that new skills are maintained once supports have been withdrawn.

There are, however, times when even with the best will in the world, the focus has to shift to the reduction of undesired behaviours; by definition these are *punishment contingencies* (see Chapter 2). Particular care has to be taken when teaching parents specific behaviour reduction methods, especially if families have long-standing difficulties or a history of abuse. For example, the use of a procedure called *time out from positive reinforcement* can easily be misconstrued. In this procedure the positive reinforcer that maintains the problem behaviour is identified and removed, in other words, timed-out. If the reinforcer cannot be identified or controlled, this procedure can involve removal of the child from any possible reinforcers; the child is temporarily removed from the setting where the problem behaviour occurred and placed in a setting where the behaviour is definitely not reinforced. All too often however, *time out from positive reinforcement* is abbreviated to 'time-out' and the child is removed simply as a 'punishment for bad behaviour'. This is NOT a behaviour analytic procedure and it is definitely NOT what *time out from positive reinforcement* is supposed to be about. The *time out from positive reinforcement* procedure involves very skilful identification of the reinforcer, for example, through a functional assessment, and the removal of this specific reinforcer from the environment so it is no longer available, thus reducing the probability of the problem behaviour recurring.

Evidently *time out from positive reinforcement* is a difficult procedure. A good behavioural parent education tutor applies the principle of least restrictive interventions and focuses on the large number of much less restrictive, highly effective procedures to reduce problem behaviours, for example, differential reinforcement of alternative, other, incompatible, competing, or low rate behaviours. Unfortunately however, *time out from positive reinforcement* can and has been misused widely by staff in different settings, for example, to exclude a child who engages in challenging behaviours for long periods of time, rather than dealing with the problem behaviour appropriately. Clearly, interventions for families where abuse or neglect is an issue must focus on improving the relationship between child and parent alongside addressing behaviour reduction techniques.

## Contextual factors

Contextual factors that impact on the effectiveness of parent education interventions include limited resources, the nature of the referral, the inaccessibility of direct observation of neglectful behaviours, and the need for interventions that target other areas of the family's life. This means that contextual factors need to be thoroughly assessed and factored into behaviour parent training programmes; a comprehensive assessment of the family's parenting skills and social networks may be necessary. Clearly, direct observation should be the main assessment technique, but given the neglect is the omission of child care behaviours, this has to be supplemented by other more indirect assessment methods, such as behavioural interviews or file searches.

It is particularly important that parent education methods are appropriately tailored to the needs of each individual family. If parents have not already developed the basic skills necessary for social communication, such as eye contact, turn taking, or smiling, they will have difficulty with reciprocal, complex, and varied interaction with their child, especially when these interactions need to be adjusted as the child develops. Of course, some of the core skills, such as being able to read instruction leaflets are important, however educational materials can be adapted, for example, pictorial manuals can be used instead of written prompts. Other interventions may be necessary to help parents deal with their own experiences of being parented, especially if they themselves experienced abuse or neglect and thus did not have 'good parenting models' in their own parents. In these cases, immediate and practical support is more effective in increasing maternal sensitivity. Behavioural interventions to increase parental sensitivity to very young babies usually focus on enhanced physical contact and may include for example, the use of soft baby carriers.

Teaching child care skills to parents with intellectual disabilities is usually quite successful, if focussed on the right target behaviours. In many cases, parents with disabilities interact less with their children than other parents, using lower rates of praise and imitation. This may be due to the fact that they are unable to read social cues from their child and consequently their children are more likely at risk of neglect. Furthermore, parents with intellectual disabilities may overtax their social support systems with demands of immediate attention. However, many parents with intellectual disabilities can learn to look after their children with appropriate supports.

For these parents in particular, behaviour parent education programmes are most effective when strategies are based on concrete rather than abstract concepts, for example, though modelling rather than instructional techniques, using tangible reinforcers that are gradually faded, constructing clear straightforward task analysis, offering frequent verbal feedback, and conducting frequent reinforcer preference assessment, as well as explicitly promoting generalisation and maintenance. In many cases, once appropriate child care skills have been learned, for example, parental responsiveness and child vocalisation have been increased beyond the levels expected due to maturation, changes can be maintained in the home environment.

In any case, workers need to be well trained to ensure interventions are carried out with integrity and fidelity. Supervision can be difficult because in order to promote generalisation and maintenance, interventions are best conducted in the family's homes where supervisors do not easily have access. Unfortunately, if programmes are not successful, it is often seen as a failure on the part of the parents rather than a failure of arranging effective individually tailored contingencies.

## Summary

Behavioural parent education offers several benefits to parents and babies who are vulnerable to neglect. First, rather than placing blame on the parents the focus is on methods of change. This anti-discriminatory approach recognises that any parent may occasionally fail to meet the basic needs of their children or occasionally avoid interaction with their child. It is when this behaviour becomes extreme and persistent that difficulties arise. Rather than looking for the causes of neglect inside the parent's mind, personality traits, or genetics, behavioural parent education searches for environmental causes of behaviour and proactive ways for change.

Second, clearly defining individually tailored target behaviours addresses the lack of collectively agreed standards of parenting. Few generally agreed standards for parenting exist and those that exist are open to interpretation. It is clearly important that child care workers have a good working knowledge of possible indicators of neglect, normal child development, as well as the impact of wider social factors. However, behavioural parent education recognises that these definitions are socially constructed and therefore that acceptable minimum standards for child care need to be culturally sensitive and agreed with parents. A close working relationship with other professionals is also beneficial to reaching a consensus on thresholds for intervention.

Within existing research on child neglect, behavioural studies stand out because of their methodological rigour and successful outcomes. Many studies have focussed particularly on parents with intellectual disabilities and have been undertaken in parents' homes. The aim of the detailed programmes reported in Chapters 6–10 was to develop methods of assessment and intervention for a wider service-user group, specifically for young vulnerable first-time mothers of babies at risk of neglect.

# CHAPTER 5

# Developing Programmes for Neglect Prevention

In the following chapters, a number of different behavioural parent education programmes are developed and evaluated. These programmes were designed to address some of the key child care skills that are necessary to provide appropriate child care and prevent child neglect:

**Chapter 6:** Child Care Skills
**Chapter 7:** Child Care Routines
**Chapter 8:** Home Safety
**Chapter 9:** Home Hygiene
**Chapter 10:** Parent–Child Interaction

The key of these programmes is not their automatic replicability. The important learning from this chapter is about the way in which these programmes were developed by first defining the target behaviours, than designing and delivering the programmes while continuously taking behavioural data and feeding the data back into the loop to improve the programme, Figure 5.1. Materials used to implement these programmes are available at the end of this book are available from www.caldertrainingandconsultancy.co.uk. It is important to modify these materials to suit the needs of families, for example to match the age and developmental needs of the child and the parent's reading abilities. Parents should also be involved in designing forms.

The setting in which these programmes were developed and delivered was a residential assessment unit for young mothers and their babies or very young children. The unit was a purpose built facility that offered individual two-bedroom apartment style accommodation for each of six mother-baby dyads that lived there at any one time. At least 2 members of support staff were present in the project at all times.

The mother-baby dyads were referred to the unit by Social Services due to concerns about the mother's child care skills, her lack of knowledge about parenting, and subsequent worries about adequate care and protection for her baby or child. The mothers' age in the project ranged from 16 to 25 years-of-age and the age of their babies and children ranged from birth to 3 years-of-age. The children were either under Care Orders or on the Child Protection Register, under the category of

neglect. Most of the mothers under 18 years-of-age were themselves subject to Care Orders or on the Child Protection Register. The focus of the project was on two areas:

1. the mother's ability to care for and protect her child;
2. the mother's ability to care for herself.

Placements usually ranged in length from 3 months to one year, although on occasion placements ended earlier, especially if there were concerns about risk to the child such that they were taken into care. All major decisions were taken at case conferences or reviews.

Of course, living in a residential setting offered a number of advantages, such as a degree of protection against poverty, one of the main factors associated with neglect. Poverty did not affect the mothers in the project to the same degree as it did while they lived in the community because they were able to avail themselves of living accommodation that was kept at a good standard and social and practical support from both staff and other residents. However, there were also drawbacks to living in residential accommodation, such as being constantly

**Figure 5.1:** Developing behaviour parent education programmes: The 4-D feedback loop (adapted from Dillenburger, 2010)

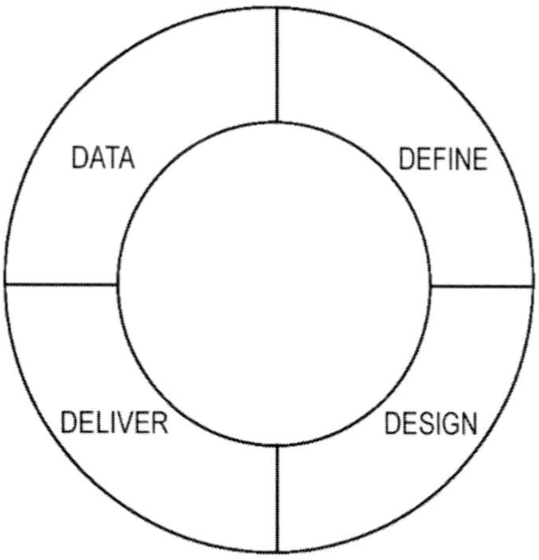

monitored and the increased sense of isolation after moving out into the community. In any case, many of the mothers did not have a choice about coming to the project, as they were there under direction from court.

The mother-baby dyads that participated in the individual behavioural parent education programmes described here also continued to receive the range of other services provided by the project. These were agreed on an individual basis prior to admission and included individual counselling, learning home-making skills, and on-going staff advice and support with child care. They were selected to take part in the additional behavioural parent education programmes on the basis of an assessed lack of basic child care skills and difficulties in home hygiene and home safety.

The programmes were developed and conducted under the auspices of the Research Governance Framework of a local university. Appropriate ethical permission was obtained and residents and staff were consulted in the design of instruments and procedures. Independent healthcare professionals reviewed the data collection instruments. The target behaviours addressed in these programmes were all part of the usual service provided by the project.

Detailed behavioural programmes were individually tailored to:

- Meet the needs of both parent and child.
- Enhance parental ability to undertake child care tasks at appropriate times.
- Enrich communication between parent and child.
- Improve parental ability to provide a safe and hygienic living environment for their children.
- Increase parental sensitivity to the child's physical and emotional needs.

Fifteen family dyads took part in the development and evaluation of the programmes described here. Further background information on individual families is given in the detailed description of each programme. Children ranged in age from birth to 3 years of age. The children in thirteen (86%) families were on the Child Protection Register under the category of neglect. Five children were subject to Care Orders. All of the families were perceived to be at high risk of neglect because of their current and previous life experiences. Table 5.1 summarises

**Table 5.1:**  Participating parent-child dyads and target skills for each dyad

| Name | Parent age | Care history | Learning difficulty | Social support | Child age | Care proceedings (child) | Child protection register | Target skills |
|------|-----------|--------------|---------------------|----------------|-----------|--------------------------|---------------------------|----------------|
| Laura | 16 | Y | N | Y | 1 week | N | Y | *Bathing* |
| Evelyn | 24 | N | Y | Y | 12 weeks | N | Y | *Bathing* <br> *Interaction* |
| Jane | 16 | Y | N | Y | 2 weeks | N | Y | *Feeding* |
| Charlotte | 18 | N | N | N | 1 week | Y | Y | *Feeding* |
| Lee | 21 | N | Y | Y | 5 months | N | Y | *Feeding* |
| Caroline | 16 | Y | N | N | 1 week | Y | Y | *Bathing* <br> *Feeding* <br> *Routines* |
| Ruby | 25 | N | N | N | 6 months | N | Y | *Bathing* <br> *Feeding* <br> *Routines* <br> *Home Hygiene* |
| Susan | 17 | | | N | 3 weeks | N | Y | *Routines* <br> *Home Hygiene* |
| Judy | 19 | N | N | Y | 18 months | N | Y | *Home Safety* |
| Lynne | 17 | Y | N | Y | 8 months | N | N | *Home Safety* |
| Karen | 20 | N | Y | Y | 1 year & 2 years | N | Y | *Home Safety* <br> *Home Hygiene* |
| Cathleen | 19 | N | N | N | 1 year & 3 years | Y | Y | *Home Safety* <br> *Home Hygiene* |
| Hannah | 17 | Y | N | Y | 2 weeks | N | N | *Home Hygiene* |
| Mary | 18 | Y | N | N | 12 weeks | N | Y | *Interaction* |
| Alice | 18 | Y | N | Y | 13 weeks | Y | Y | *Interaction* |

the parent-child dyads that took part in the programmes and identifies the targeted child care skills.

Mothers who participated in the programmes, had experienced difficult childhoods, interrupted schooling and/or intellectual disabilities, frequent moves, involvement with social services, lack of experience of independent living, early parenthood, and limited support from partners/social isolation.

*Difficult childhoods*: All participating mothers experienced maltreatment when they were children. This included one or more of the following: neglect and/or physical, emotional or sexual abuse. Just over half of mothers had lived in local authority care for more than two years. As a result of these childhood experiences many mothers had limited exposure to consistent or positive parenting. Although the majority of mothers continued to have contact with their families, in many cases this was not supportive.

*Interrupted schooling or intellectual disabilities*: Multiple moves throughout the care system or difficult home circumstances meant that many of the mothers did not attend school regularly. As a result these mothers often had poor literacy skills, few qualifications and subsequently very limited job prospects. Three of the mothers were classed as having mild or borderline intellectual disabilities and had received a Statement of Special Educational Needs (SSEN) while they were still at school. Others had not received a SSEN because of poor school attendance, which meant that they had not been able to access specialist educational services. Some of these mothers were retrospectively assessed as having intellectual disabilities as a result of psychological assessment requested by child care workers or the courts because there were serious concerns about care for the baby. It is possible that other participating mothers had undiagnosed intellectual disabilities.

*Frequent moves*: Most of the mothers who had been in care had experienced many moves through a variety of settings including children's homes, foster homes, and secure accommodation. Even those mothers who had remained in the care of their families had experienced frequent moves during early adolescence, such as moving to live with other family members or friends to escape difficult or abusive home circumstances. Nine mothers (60%) had experienced three or more moves in the eighteen months prior to coming to the project. In addition, some of the young

mothers who had grown up in care experienced periods of homelessness after they had left local authority care. As a consequence of these disruptions, most of these young mothers had become socially isolated, had unpredictable lifestyles with little in way of routines for activities such as sleeping or eating and thus found it difficult to provide routines for their babies.

*Involvement with social services*: Most of the participating young mothers had been involved with social services since childhood. As a result professionals monitored the mother's ability to parent more closely than would have been the case with other young parents. As mentioned earlier, at least three of the young mothers had intellectual disabilities, which resulted in high levels of professional concern and close monitoring. Perhaps not surprisingly, these mothers did not always see child care service involvement as supportive; in fact, many were resentful of any professional involvement.

*Lack of experience of independent living*: The majority of the young mothers did not have positive experiences of living alone and lacked basic life skills, such as budgeting, shopping, cooking, establishing a social network, or maintaining a home. While this may be the same for any adolescent leaving home, others usually have both emotional and practical support from their birth families. Young care leavers usually do not have family support and with the extra responsibility of caring for a baby the participating mothers were doubly disadvantaged.

*Early parenthood*: Teenage mothers are three times more likely to develop post-natal depression and their children are at risk of lower birth weights and higher infant mortality rates than older mothers. The age of the mothers in the programmes reported here ranged from 16 to 25 years-of-age; the average age was 18 years-of-age, and almost half the mothers were under 18 years old. Young women leaving care, who are homeless, who have underachieved at school and are themselves children of teenage parents, or live in socially deprived areas are more likely to become pregnant at a young age.

Negative stereotypes prevail towards teenage parents in a way that is not true for other mothers. Teenage pregnancy is viewed as inherently problematic and Government policies aim to reduce teenage pregnancies. In fact, between 1998 and 2008, in the UK teenage (15–17 years of age) conception rate fell from approx. 4.7% to 4.1%. Conception between 13–15 years of age remained at around 0.8%. Still, 'the UK has the highest teenage birth and abortion rates in Western Europe. Rates of teenage births are five times those in the Netherlands, double those in France and more than twice those in Germany' (FPA, 2013).

*Limited support from partners and social isolation*: Although fathers were not allowed to be resident in the project in which the programmes were conducted, they were (where possible) involved in the assessment process. Eleven of the mothers had no contact with the father of their baby. Four of the participating mothers had a relationships with the father of their child, however in one case the father had restricted contact with his child because of concerns about sexual abuse; two fathers were not allowed any contact because of domestic violence and the fourth father visited infrequently because he lived some distance from the project. Eight of the mothers (53%) had experienced domestic violence in some cases resulting in serious injury.

Six mothers were socially isolated, in other words, they did not receive any support from family or friends, relying almost entirely on professionals in the project for social contact, although three of these mothers had some contact with one or both of their own parents, the baby's grandparents. However, rather than offering support with child care, these grandparents were considered a contributing factor to the existing child protection issues, including concerns about child sex abuse and supplying drugs to the young mother.

## Data collection instruments and measures

Individual data collection instruments and assessment checklists are described in detail under each programme. In brief, assessment instruments for feeding and bathing and parent-child interaction were adapted from the criterion-based tests used at Surrey Place Project in Ontario for direct observation of child care tasks such as feeding, bottle making, nappy changing, and home safety (Feldman & Case, 1993). Assessment instruments used for routines were based on practice experience within the project, and assessment instruments used for home safety and home hygiene were based on materials developed by Project 12-Ways that were used to evaluate the impact of intervention aimed at improving conditions in the home (Watson-Perczel, Lutzker, Greene & McGimpsey, 1988).

All assessment instruments were designed to fit within the normal working process of the project and to be completed by staff and the young mothers themselves. To ensure cultural and developmental relevance and social validity, each instrument was reviewed by residents and staff and field tested with residents who were considered competent at each task. Adaptations were made as necessary.

Not all families required all of the intervention programmes. The use of developmentally sensitive instruments meant that programmes were selected individually for each family depending on the developmental level and needs of the child; for example, supervision and safety programmes became more important once the child could crawl or walk; feeding programmes that involved solid foods became relevant only once a child was old enough to be fed solid food.

In order for assessments to be adapted for individuals while still providing comparable scores, a task analysis was conducted on each target skill and measured as 'percent correct' in each programme; this was calculated by dividing the total score by the maximum possible score multiplied by 100.

## Evaluation designs

Single System Research Designs (SSRD) were selected appropriate to each programme. SSRDs are specifically designed to demonstrate the effectiveness of individually tailored interventions through repeated measurements taken before, during, and after intervention. Single-system designs can be evaluative, showing that change took place during intervention, or experimental, demonstrating that improvement was due to intervention.

Single-system designs offer three different types of knowledge. First, they offer detailed immediate quantitative accounts of the target behaviour at all stages of the intervention. Second, they offer correlational information, obtained by comparison of quantitative behavioural data on each stage of the intervention. Third, they offer causal information regarding intervention and behaviour. In the programmes described here, the information obtained using SSRDs was used to give feedback to service users about progress during the intervention or, if an intervention was not effective, to demonstrate where changes needed to be made.

Although originating from behaviour analytic research, SSRDs are not linked to a specific theoretical, psychological or educational orientation. In fact, SSRDs enable or enhance a systematic approach to assessment, goal setting and monitoring, and allow for continuous assessment (Dillenburger, 1998). They allow child care workers to evaluate the impact of interventions and base decisions about methods of work on empirical evidence of effectiveness rather than the personal preferences.

In order to undertake SSRDs it is necessary to operationally define the target behaviour in a way that allows measurement through the use of valid and reliable tools such as observation, self-report, or physiological measures. The target behaviour is clearly defined when high levels of inter-observer agreement (IOA) are reached, in other words, when at least two independent observers agree if and when the target response has occurred (Keenan et al., 2003).

Once a target behaviour is identified and clearly defined a decision has to be taken regarding the dimension on which the behaviour is to be observed. Basic dimensions include frequency (number of responses), duration (length of response in terms of time), latency (time between antecedent, for example, instruction and response), inter-response time (time between one response and the next), or intensity, a more subjective measure usually given on a Likert scale.

A baseline is established by measuring the target behaviour along the dimension that suits best the issues to be addressed, for example, if a parent does not feed her baby often enough, the number of times (frequency) a baby gets fed may be a good behavioural dimension to target, however if she feeds the baby often enough but each time feeding only lasts a few minutes, in other words, the baby does not have enough time to ingest enough food, the duration of feeding (length of time taken to feed) may be a better measure.

Taking a stable baseline is an important first step in any SSRD. It serves to show the initial severity of the problem and to monitor progress; in other words, the baseline provides a measure of the target behaviour, as it would be expected to continue if there is no intervention (Dillenburger, 1998). In some cases, for example, where very good file records are available, it may be possible to take a retrospective baseline. This is especially useful if intervention cannot be delayed to allow the collection of baseline measures, however this

can be unreliable unless based on existing concrete measures, such school attendance records. In some cases it is only necessary to take brief baseline measures if behaviour is rarely emitted, however in every case the baseline should be measured until it is 'stable', in other words, until there are no significant upward or downward trends in the baseline. Unstable baselines do not allow for adequate conclusions about the effectiveness of the intervention; an upward slope in the baseline may mean that the target response already is affected by events in the environment that have nothing to do with the intervention.

There are a range of SSRDs and the selection of which design to use for a specific intervention depends on a number of factors. For a simple 'AB' design, a baseline (the 'A' phase) is taken and then the effect of the intervention (the 'B' phase) is measured to illustrate that change has happened. Obviously, a simple AB design cannot give definite information about the cause of change because it is not fully controlled, in other words, the change in behaviour at B could have occurred for a range of different reasons; the AB design also cannot demonstrate that change has been maintained.

More complex single-system designs such as ABAB reversal designs, multiple-baseline designs, or changing criterion designs are required to prove that an intervention and nothing else is responsible for the change. In an ABAB reversal design (Figure 5.2) the baseline (A) is taken followed by the implementation of an intervention (B), then the intervention is temporarily withdrawn for a brief return to baseline (A) before the intervention (B) is reinstated. If the return to baseline shows behaviour returning to levels that are similar to the original baseline, this is considered a demonstration that it was the intervention and nothing else that affected the behavioural change during the intervention phase and consequently, the probability that explanations that lie outside the intervention are greatly reduced. Clearly, an ABAB reversal design provides good evidence of the effectiveness of an intervention and therefore may be useful in 'experimental' settings, however the obvious disadvantage of ABAB designs in real life settings is that practically speaking a return to baseline may not be desired or ethical, especially if the socially relevant target behaviour was achieved during the intervention, as this would mean withdrawing an intervention that appears to be working. However, there are times, when

**Figure 5.2:**   ABAB reversal design

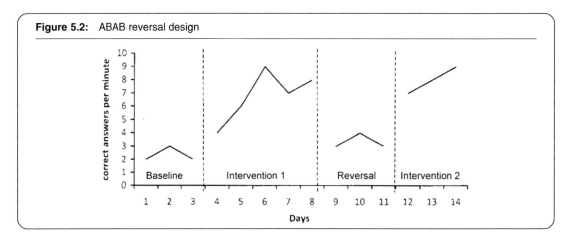

naturally occurring events necessitate a withdrawal or withholding of an intervention, such as a holiday period or a child's sickness. In these cases it makes sense to continue to take data on the target responses and thus take advantage of the naturally occurring return to baseline conditions. However, this is not always possible and other SSRDs may be more appropriate.

A multiple baseline design across behaviours records a number of target behaviours using baselines of different lengths, with interventions implemented successively, one at a time. The expectation is that only the behaviour that is targeted by the intervention changes, while all the other baseline measures remain stable until an intervention is introduced that is specifically focussed on the next behaviour. Measures are also taken after each intervention has finished and can show that changes have been maintained. Multiple baseline designs can also be taken across situations or environments. This time, the same behaviour is measured during baselines in different situations, for example, a specific 'stimming' behaviour is measured in the kitchen, the living room, and in school. Successive implementation of the intervention means that first the stimming response is targeted in the kitchen, while baseline data are still taken in the living room and the school and these baselines are expected to remain stable. Once the intervention effect is observed in the kitchen, the behaviour is targeted in the living room and again, baseline data records are continued at school. Once the intervention in the living room is evidently effective, an intervention is implemented in the school environment. Multiple baseline designs can also be taken across participants, in other words, the same target behaviour is observed in

the same situations across a number of different participants. Again interventions are implemented sequentially while baseline data are recorded for non-targeted participants.

Multiple baseline designs can demonstrate that change occurred only when the specific intervention was introduced and therefore that intervention was responsible for changes in behaviour and not something else. There are certain drawbacks to multiple-baseline designs particularly because withholding intervention for an extended baseline may be unethical and impractical. It also may be difficult to establish effectiveness, if some behaviours in a programme improve and others do not. On the other hand, sometimes the baselines for non-targeted behaviours change prior to the implementation of intervention for that particular behaviour. While this may be welcomed as a sign that generalisation is happening without further intervention it does hinder the assumption that the intervention, and nothing else, effected the behaviour change.

In a changing-criterion design, no baseline measures are required. Instead, the criterion is gradually increased in steps toward the required rates of the target behaviour; in other words, each 'step' serves as a baseline for the following step (Figure 7.1 in Chapter 7 shows an example of this design). In a sense the changing criterion design monitors the shaping process of achieving the final target behaviour through successive approximations. Once the target criterion is reached at one step, the criterion is increased until the final target behaviour is reached. Obvious benefits of this design are that early success is reinforced as each criterion level is reached and the target response rate is achieved in gradual steps. This design does not require an extended baseline, which is useful when intervention cannot be delayed, for example, when dealing with life sustaining child care tasks such as feeding or home safety. It also does not require a return to baseline, which has ethical as well as practical downsides. However, there are difficulties in evaluating behaviour that does not match criterion levels. Changing criterion designs therefore only allow the evaluation of interventions that can be designed with changes in performance being implemented stepwise.

Regardless of the design that is chosen to monitor a specific intervention, it is vital that data are gathered regarding generalisation of target responses to other situations or in the presence of other staff or family members. Equally important are the data that are taken at follow-up to ensure that any changes in behaviour are maintained and do not only happening during the intervention phase. Generalisation and behaviour maintenance cannot be assumed by-products of intervention. They require specific planning and the inclusion of generalisation and maintenance procedures in every behaviour parent education programme.

Clearly, the use of single-system research designs improves practice because it ensures that goals are identified together with the service user, are explicit and clearly defined and progress is recorded systematically to allows for immediate change in ineffective interventions. Of course it is important also to record other aspects of the service user's situation so that SSRDs are suited to the context of the service user. In the context of the programmes reported here a number of different SSRDs were used to suit the context and target behaviour for each mother-baby dyad.

## Programme design and procedures

Designing individualised programmes is the hallmark of applied behaviour analysis. In the programme descriptions that follow, each programme began with an initial assessment meeting with the mother, field child care worker, and keyworker from the project to identify target areas for intervention. Baseline measures of basic child care skills outlined in the first programme provided information for the identification of specific target areas of child care. Staff and individual mothers agreed criterion levels for each task. When criterion levels were met intervention moved onto another area of child care. If criterion levels were not reached, external factors were

explored, criterion levels were renegotiated, and the programme was reviewed and adjusted as necessary.

Assessment and intervention were divided into five areas:

1. Child Care Skills.
2. Child Care Routines.
3. Home Safety.
4. Home Hygiene.
5. Parent–Child Interaction.

These areas were selected based on the fact that many young mothers in the project had difficulties with these skills and there was evidence that these areas were closely related to adverse outcomes for children, including neglect.

A number of behaviour analytic principles were used throughout the programmes, including a combination of verbal and written prompts, modelling, and positive reinforcement in the form of a token economy system. Vouchers were used as tokens throughout intervention to reinforce target behaviours. Vouchers then could be exchanged at a later stage for a range of items or activities. One of the main advantages of using tokens was that reinforcers were initially offered with minimal delay and were gradually reduced once the behaviour was established. Vouchers also had the advantage that they provided variety, thus increasing effectiveness and avoiding satiation. Furthermore, vouchers were delivered immediately after the target behaviour as immediate reinforcers have been found to be more effective than delayed reinforcers, in other words, vouchers acted as a bridge and in fact became conditioned reinforcers in their own right.

A reinforcer menu was drawn up in collaboration with the mothers to ensure a sufficient variety of reinforcers were available and to allow individual mothers to add personally preferred reinforcers. One voucher was awarded for participating in each baseline observation, and during intervention, two vouchers were given for reaching a target score. If there were difficulties in reaching target behaviours, they were broken down into 'smaller' steps and additional bonus vouchers were awarded for reaching each approximation. No vouchers were awarded during the follow-up phase. In sum, the voucher system:

- Focussed on and positively reinforced progress towards the target behaviour.
- Ensured consistence across settings, monitoring and reviewing goals.

• Cued staff to reinforce and thus encourage target behaviours.

Vouchers were given for participation in the assessment process regardless of whether or not a mother was included in a specific programme.

Clearly, it is important that newly learned child care behaviours were reinforced within natural contingencies so that behaviour changes were maintained when mothers and children move into the community. Therefore, vouchers were gradually phased out once target behaviours were established and replaced by more naturally occurring reinforcers, for example, verbal praise by staff and self-praise. Reducing the vouchers meant that reinforcement was changed from a continuous to an intermittent schedule. Remember, a continuous schedule occurs when every occurrence of a target behaviour is reinforced and is useful for establishing target behaviours; in intermittent schedules only occasional responses are reinforced and these schedules are used to maintain established behaviour, particularly when paired with naturally occurring reinforcers.

## Data analysis

Quantitative measures of target behaviours along specified dimensions, for example, frequency, duration, latency, inter-response time, are important, both as evidence of outcomes and to demonstrate progress. For this purpose, line graphs allowed for objective visual analysis of data because they were based on concrete measures rather than the subjective interpretation of idiosyncratic observations of a child care worker (Cooper et al., 2007). Graphs were easily understood and therefore shared with parents and workers to evaluate progress.

A number of single-system research designs were utilised in the programmes and consequently, data collected before, during and after each programme were presented in line graphs for the visual analysis of effectiveness of each programme. Graphing raw data after each observation session demonstrated effectively the impact of intervention and identified when procedures needed to be adapted. Visual analysis identified quickly whether or not changes in the target behaviour had taken place during intervention and repeated baselines evidenced whether or not the intervention was responsible for the change.

## Ethical considerations

The basic ethics of behavioural parent education and child care skills development are the same as those of anti-oppressive child care practice generally. Moreover, because interventions that are based on behaviour analysis have been shown to be more effective than others, they generally engender a higher level of effectiveness, accountability, and social validity than approaches that have not been empirically tested (Dillenburger, 1998).

In point of fact, behavioural parent education extends child care ethics in that it views difficulties in parenting not as faults of the parent, but instead analyses them as skill deficits within a wider environmental, cultural, and historical context. Thus behavioural parent education does not blame or label mothers, instead it looks at parenting skills and offers methods of change that remove the stigma of being seen as a failure as a parent.

Parental empowerment is central to the ethics of behavioural parent education, in other words, parents learn to maximise the quality of life for themselves and their families (Adams, 2003). The question of the direction of change, in other words, which behaviours were targeted in a specific programme was addressed in partnership with the parent prior to the implementation of the programme. The decision was made following discussions between the child care worker and the parent or caregiver. Although the power difference in child protection work cannot be avoided completely, agreeing shared goals and methods of work allowed for clarity about what was expected.

Ethics governing behavioural work include the right of the individual to the most effective intervention available (Van Houten et al., 1987). Behaviour analysts therefore have a responsibility to use evidence-based techniques that have been shown to be effective and they have to evaluate the on-going work so that intervention can be adapted when it was not effective. Through commitment to respect for human dignity, openness and fairness, informed consent and confidentiality, the best interests of the services user is to the fore. These interests are also served by establishing the best available evidence, social validity, and evaluation of effectiveness of intervention and the avoidance of potentially harmful effects.

The programmes described here were conducted in line with the Research Governance

Framework of a local University, the British Association of Social Workers (BASW) Code of Ethics (BASW, 2011) and the BACB Guidelines for Responsible Conduct for Behavior Analysts (BACB, 2012).

Informed consent was obtained from all families prior to the start of the programmes (Data Protection Act, 1998). The information and consent session took place in the mothers' flat in the presence of a child care worker. Where necessary, information and consent sheets were read out by staff, for example, for parents who had literacy problems. The information sheet assured mothers that participation in the programmes was voluntary and services 'as usual' were maintained for anyone who did not want to take part. Consent also included agreement to direct observation by staff, which was already routine work practice in the facility and therefore mothers were used to staff coming into their flats for monitoring visits. All of the families who were invited to take part consented.

With regard to confidentiality, names were changed and distinguishing features were omitted, so that participants could not be identified. Internally within the facility, the outcomes of the programmes formed part of the overall assessment of parenting and the information from the programme evaluation contributed toward the determination of care arrangements for the child.

Mothers contributed to their personal data recording and were able to view their own data at any time; obviously individual family data were not shared with other families. Video recordings were stored securely, viewed only by authorised observers, and given to the mother at the end of her placement in the facility.

Children's rights were protected through the agency and statutory safeguarding procedures. Although decisions about children's futures were not based entirely on the assessment outcomes detailed in the programmes reported here, they did contribute significantly to the overall assessment. Mother's privacy was respected, for example, observation sessions were arranged at agreed times and only the mother, child, and child care professionals were present during programme sessions.

A note of caution: some of the mothers who participated in the programmes had an extremely difficult childhood and upbringing themselves and oftentimes found parenting very difficult. As such they were substantially more vulnerable and thus not entirely representative of young parents generally, many of who are able to parent their children very successfully.

Only four of the participant mothers had partners but none of the fathers took part in the programmes. Two of the fathers were actively involved in their children's lives and initially attended the meetings but did not become involved in the full programmes. The other two fathers had engaged in domestic violence against the mother and did not have any contact with their children; consequently, they declined offers of contact with child care staff and did not get involved in the programme.

## Task analysis

A task analysis is a list of all the behaviours and skills that are necessary to complete a specific task. Depending on the task or skill, task analyses are constructed either in sequential or random order. A task analysis involves the clear and concrete stepwise description of all the behaviours a person has to be able to complete competently, in order to achieve a final outcome. A task analysis therefore can be conducted for any task, not just child care tasks. Life skills, such as making a cup of tea, doing the dishes, or cooking a meal can easily be broken down into a step-by-step task analysis (Keenan & Dillenburger, 2012). Task analyses for the programmes described here were based on adapted versions of Step-by-Step Child Care (Feldman & Case, 1993).

In order to ensure task analyses were of the standards expected within the project, two residents who were competent in the relevant child care tasks were observed. A record of their behaviour was transcribed into a stepwise task analysis. The task analysis checklists were assessed against child care literature to ensure that no safety steps had been omitted and a professionally qualified, highly experienced health visitor reviewed the checklists. Finally, the list of steps was discussed with the residents whose child care behaviour had been observed to ensure that each step was socially valid, acceptable, easily understood, and free from jargon. A member of staff re-enacted each task analysis to ensure that the steps followed a logical sequence. This process was video recorded for use in staff training.

For some skills more than one task analysis was necessary in order to be sensitive to the child's age, for example, two bathing checklists were drawn up, one for young babies who used a small baby bath tub and the other for older children who could bath in the 'big' bath tub in the bathroom. Checklists also were individualised if a mother had an equally safe but idiosyncratic method of carrying out a child care task and additional steps were added as necessary in agreement with the mother, for example, one child had to receive medication with feeds and needed to be fed in a specific way because of swallowing problems.

Steps in the task analysis that did not apply to individual mothers were scored as N/A and omitted from the final scoring, for example if a mother chose not to use moisturising cream for her baby after the bath. Obviously, essential safety steps, such as checking the temperature of the milk in the bottle or the water in the bath tub and ensuring that the baby was in a safe place were never excluded. The step 'mother looks at the baby and maintains eye contact' while undertaking the task was included in all checklists. General observations were noted as field notes and comments for further information on the observation, often in relation to events that prevented the mother from fully completing the task. After the baseline phase, these comments were shared with the mothers as part of the intervention procedure.

A task analysis can be used for three different intervention procedures; *Total Task Presentation*; *Backward Chaining*; and *Forward Chaining*. In Total Task Presentation, the parent is taught to complete the whole task, in other words, to complete the whole chain of behaviour in 'one go'. In chaining, parents are taught one step at a time, while the member of staff completes the remainder of the steps. In Backward Chaining the staff member starts the sequence and the parent initially completes only the final step. Once they are competent in this final step they complete the last two steps, then the last three steps, etc., until they are able to complete the whole task. In Forward Chaining, the parent is taught the first step first, while the staff member completes the remainder of the task. Once the parent is competent in the first step, the parent completes the first two steps, then the first three etc. until the parent completes the whole task adeptly. There are good clinical reasons why one of these procedures may be chosen above the others for a specific task analysis based intervention. For example, when teaching a child to get dressed, Backward Chaining usually is very successful. In Backward Chaining the child

starts by completing the last step, for example, when learning how to put on trousers, the parent starts the sequence by putting both of the child's legs into the trouser legs but the child pulls the trouser up herself, thus completing the task and earning the natural reinforcer, such as parental praise for a job well done.

## Training for observers

Staff members in the project were trained as observers in the use of all assessment instruments. Training sessions were carried out with small groups of staff and lasted a total of eight hours. This training included an introduction to basic behavioural principles, familiarisation of how to use the child care checklists, and test scoring of the video of a member of staff completing each of the child care tasks. This was repeated until everyone scored the video 80% correct. Knowledge of behavioural principles was tested in a written test and all participants scored above 85%. Follow-up training was conducted informally when necessary throughout the programmes. Written guidelines were provided on how to complete assessments.

Formal inter-observer reliability checks were not possible, because observations took place in mothers' flats as part of the normal work process. However, only those staff trained in the use of checklists undertook observations. The scoring was discussed and agreed with each mother immediately afterwards.

Baseline measures were taken for all mothers on all these child care behaviours using the task analysis to identify required behaviours and the scoring checklists to identify if a mother had engaged in these required behaviours or not. Mothers who achieved a score above 80% on three occasions in a particular child care skill, in other words, met the criterion level for 'being able to engage in the task fluently' without need for intervention, did not undertake the programme that targeted that particular skill. Mothers who scored below criterion level during baseline, performing <80% of the task analysis steps correctly, were included in the relevant programme.

Each behaviour parent education programme described in this section addressed specific significant areas of child care that are relevant for the prevention of child neglect. These include basic child care skills, child care routines, home safety, home hygiene, and parent-child interaction. These programmes are not 'off the shelf' instructions or manuals or specific curricula. They are examples of how to apply behaviour analytic knowledge to vulnerable families of children at risk of neglect to develop evidence-based strategies to develop child care skills. These examples enable child care practitioners to understand how to develop and evaluate behaviour parent education strategies that are individually tailored to the families with whom they work.

# CHAPTER 6

# Child Care Skills

The previous programme focussed on two specific child care skills, feeding and bathing a baby, and took place in the residential facility. This meant that rather than creating arbitrary role-plays in a clinical setting, the programmes were implemented in-vivo and in-situ. In order to ensure validity and reliability, the programme was replicated with seven families.

The child care skills programme built on work by Feldman and colleagues (1993) who developed skills-based parent education methods for parents with intellectual disabilities. The programme included task analyses of both child care tasks. At the most basic level, a task analysis is a list of all the component skills that are necessary for the successful completion a more complex skill, in other words, a task analysis sets out the chain of behaviours that lead to a final target behaviour. Practice Tool 1 includes an exercise that can be used by practitioners to develop task analyses. These can be adapted to be used for a range of different child care behaviours

Practice Tool 1 shows the task analysis for bathing and feeding a baby that were used in this programme. Both of these complex child care behaviours were broken down into simple component skills steps. These task analyses were developed through careful observations of parents who lived in the project and who were considered competent in each of these child care behaviours. Staff and parents validated these task analyses as reflecting the necessary steps/skills to complete each of the tasks appropriately and competently. The lists in the Practice Tools are meant to be examples, rather than definitive and will need to be adjusted to the context of the family with whom they are used.

This programme used forward chaining, modelling, and social reinforcement to enhance basic physical care of infants and to assess if skill-deficit based neglect in these areas can be addressed through skills training.

At the time this programme was implemented none of the participating children were diagnosed with failure to thrive, however, there was concern about their weight and feeding patterns and the participating mother had scored below 80% on the assessment of these child care skills. Irregular, inconsistent, and inadequate feeding routines clearly have implications that go beyond weight gain. They can lead to problems in physical, mental, and emotional development. Effective intervention during the first year of life brings benefits both in the short and long term.

Seven mother-child dyads took part in the feeding and bathing programme, including three boys and four girls. All of the children were officially registered at risk of neglect; two of the children were also registered at risk of physical or sexual abuse from other family members, including their fathers. The mothers were called Laura, Evelyn, Jane, Charlotte, Lee, Caroline, and Ruby (not their real names).

## Laura

Laura was taken into care when she was 3 years of age after she had been sexually abused by a family member. She grew up in a foster home until she was 14 years of age, when the placement broke down and she experienced several moves including an admission to a children's residential unit and a short period in supported accommodation. Laura was 16 years of age when she moved into the project and had just given birth to her first baby. She was still subject of a care order herself. The father of the baby was supportive but lived 40 miles away from the project and contact with him was limited. Laura had regular contact with some of her birth family. Laura's baby was 1 week old and she took part in the bathing skills programme.

## Evelyn

Evelyn came to the attention of Social Services at 24 years of age, when her first baby was born. Evelyn had intellectual disabilities and had never lived independently. Although Evelyn had a Statement of Special Educational Needs, she was not deemed eligible for adult disability services. Having attended a residential school, Evelyn had very limited experience with children but she hadregular contact and on-going support from her family. Evelyn's baby was 12 weeks old and she took part in the bathing skills programme.

## Jane

Jane was subject to a Care Order. Her family had been known to Social Services for many years because of concerns about neglect in relation to Jane herself. Jane was 16 years of age when she was referred to the project because of domestic violence perpetrated by a much older partner. Jane had regular contact with family and friends. Her baby was 2 weeks old and she took part in the feeding programme.

## Charlotte

Charlotte's family was known to Social Services because of concerns about neglect and sexual abuse against Charlotte herself when she was a child. Charlotte was 18 years of age and had two children. Her older child had been freed for adoption due to evidence of neglect. Charlotte was referred to the project because of concerns about the impact of her lifestyle on her child. Charlotte's baby was 1 week old. Charlotte drank and smoked heavily during her pregnancy and consequently the baby had a serious medical condition. Charlotte's birth family included a number of convicted sex offenders. Her contact with the family was restricted to 2 nights supervised access that did not include the baby, who was placed with foster carers for the duration of Charlotte's family visits. Charlotte took part in the feeding programme.

## Lee

Lee's family had a long history of involvement with Social Services because of the neglect that Lee herself experienced when she was a child. Lee was 21 years of age and living with her birth family prior to moving to the project. Lee had intellectual disabilities and no experience of independent living, but had expressed a desire to live independently in the community with her child. Lee was not eligible for adult disability services. Lee's baby was 5 months old and it was unclear how much child care Lee had been undertaking herself while she was living with her birth family. Professionals involved with the family were concerned that Lee's mother had been completing most child care tasks. Lee continued to have regular contact with her family following admission. She was involved in the feeding programme.

## Caroline

Caroline was taken into care at 2 years of age because of neglect she experienced herself as a baby. Caroline remained with foster parents until she was 13 years of age when the placement broke down because the foster parents were unable to manage Caroline's disruptive behaviour. Caroline moved house a number of times before being admitted to the project prior to the birth of her first baby. Caroline's baby did not gain weight at the expected rate and was referred to a paediatrician who found no physical reason for the lack of weight gain. Caroline had occasional contact with her family but felt rejected by them. Caroline's baby was placed with foster parents for weekend respite on a fortnightly basis. Caroline took part in the bathing and feeding programmes. She also took part in the child care routine programme described later.

## Ruby

Since the death of her mother when Ruby was 15 years of age, Ruby had moved frequently between homeless hostels and several unsuccessful attempts at independent living. Ruby was 25 years old and had 2 children. Her older child was freed for adoption as the result of serious concerns about neglect. Ruby's second child was born prematurely but there were no serious health issues. The family health visitor reported that the baby's weight gain was slower than expected. Ruby was admitted to the project when her baby was 6 months old. Ruby had infrequent family contact, which often resulted in arguments. Ruby also had occasional contact with the father of her baby leading to incidents of domestic violence. Ruby had no social network; her only social contacts were professionals. Ruby took part in the bathing and feeding programme. She also took part in the child care routines and home hygiene programmes described later.

## Materials

Task analyses of bathing and feeding were used in this programme. Feeding was selected because of the importance of this skill in ensuring the overall health and development of infants. Concerns about weight gain had been raised for two out of the seven children who participated in the programme. Bathing was selected as the second skill because mothers in the project often were anxious about bathing their babies and welcomed staff support while carrying out this task. Both these skills offered mothers the opportunity to interact and develop a relationship with their babies.

Relevant materials were available for feeding, including bottles, sterilisers, and baby milk formula, and for bathing, including a baby bathtub, water, soap and shampoo, and towels.

## Procedure

Observations took place in the mother's flat at the time the mother usually carried out the task and were conducted by the member of child care staff on duty. Observations lasted for the duration of the task. During the baseline phase residents were asked to carry out tasks as normal. Staff prompted mothers if an essential safety step was omitted during baseline observations, no other feedback was offered other than thanking the mother for allowing the observation to take place. Although prompts may have had an influence on the baseline observations, they were essential to ensure the safety and wellbeing of the children. The number of baseline sessions for both skills ranged from one to three depending on the urgency for intervention and work schedules. One voucher was awarded for participating in each observation sessions during the baseline phase and two vouchers were awarded when criterion levels were reached during intervention.

For the monitoring and evaluation of the bathing programme a multiple-baseline across participants research design with follow-up (Dillenburger, 1998) was used with four mothers, although follow-up data were not available for one of the mothers. For the monitoring and evaluation of the feeding programme a multiple-baseline across participants research design with follow-up was used with five mothers, with a period of booster sessions during follow-up for two of the mothers.

The primary measure was the percentage of correctly completed steps in the task analysis. This percentage was calculating as follows:

$$\frac{\text{Total number of steps completed without prompts} \times 100}{\text{Total number of steps} - \text{steps scored as N/A}}$$

A step was scored as correctly completed if it was carried out as described on the checklist. If a step was completed following a prompt it was scored as incorrect.

The intervention procedure consisted of the following:

1. Verbal prompts were given during intervention for any missing steps, with praise given for steps completed correctly.
2. Staff modelled specific components of the task if the mother did not complete steps following a verbal prompt.
3. Checklists and scores were reviewed and the importance of missing steps was discussed with the mother, referring as necessary to child care literature.
4. Vouchers and praise were used as reinforcers for reaching 80% of correctly completed steps during intervention phase. Vouchers were not used during follow-up observations.
5. Vouchers were used to 'buy' items from a reinforcer menu.

The intervention phase continued until mothers completed 80% of the task without prompts on two successive occasions for bathing and on three successive occasions for feeding, including safety steps. Intervention for feeding was extended because of the difficulty some mothers had in reaching criterion levels. Observation sessions lasted for the length of time it took to complete the task and were followed by praise for steps completed correctly and identification of steps that had been missed. Follow-up observations for bathing took place weekly and follow-up observations of feeding took place on a daily basis.

## Results – Bathing

The skills of all four mothers who took part in the bathing programme improved to above criterion levels during intervention; see for example results for Evelyn in Figure 6.1. Three mothers reached criterion of 80% correct after only one baseline

**Figure 6.1:**   Percentage of correct responding on task analysis for bathing during baseline, intervention and follow-up for Evelyn

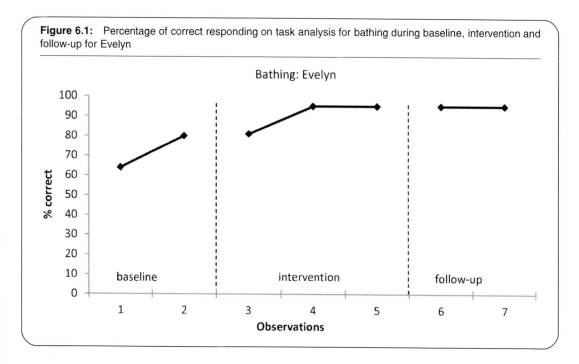

observation suggesting that the minor safety prompts during the baseline were effective in changing behaviour without the addition of praise or vouchers. Follow-up observations were completed for three mothers and showed that skills had been maintained above criterion level. As Ruby was having difficulties in all areas of child care during the period of follow-up observation and avoided staff contact by changing bath times that had been pre-arranged for observations, follow-up observations were not completed.

### Results – Feeding

The feeding programme was not as successful as the bathing programme. Although all mothers reached the target criterion of above 80% correct on three successive occasions, progress was maintained only for Jane and Lee. In fact, Jane reached and maintained criterion levels after only one baseline observation. She missed only two steps, 'discarding the milk left in the bottle' and 'rinsing out the bottle', but these did not directly affect the baby during the observed feeding session.

Ruby initially responded slowly to intervention and criterion levels were not maintained at follow-up. Some improvement occurred following a further booster session; however, Ruby was

coming to the end of her placement and was discharged before the end of the programme therefore further data were not available (see Figure 6.2). General field note comments on Ruby's observation sheets highlighted that Ruby was frequently distracted during feeds, often watching television, talking to staff about herself, or walking around. This meant that Ruby's interaction with the baby was limited while feeding and during 29% of feeding observations Ruby did not talk to or look at the baby at all. On other occasions staff noted that when Ruby did talk to the baby this was in the form of commands. Other staff comments included concerns about the baby's clothes being too small and bottles not being washed properly. A further problem was the erratic pattern of Ruby's feeding of her baby. Frequently, long periods passed between feeds and Ruby informed staff that the baby 'wasn't hungry'. Ruby responded well to praise, but became angry if staff tried to address any child care issues with her and subsequently tried to avoid staff observing feeding by changing the baby's feeding times.

Charlotte's baby had a reflux problem, which meant that additional steps were added to her task analysis in line with medical advice. The baby required medication and a nappy change before being given a bottle; furthermore, medical instruction stated that she was to be given the full

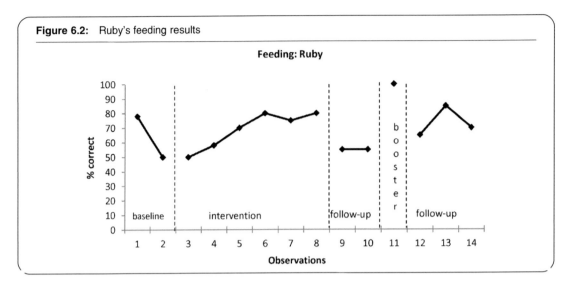

**Figure 6.2:**  Ruby's feeding results

bottle before winding. For Charlotte's baby it was particularly important that steps were followed in exact sequence, and consequently Charlotte's task of feeding was more complex than for the other mothers.

Charlotte's feeding behaviour improved initially following baseline observations but progress was not maintained. Charlotte had to be prompted during 36% of the observations to administer medication before feeding. Although at one stage Charlotte scored above criterion levels over three successive observations, this was not maintained at follow up. Staff field note comments indicated that Charlotte was at times distracted during feeds, often watching television. On other occasions Charlotte was quiet and withdrawn. During 59% of all observations Charlotte did not talk to or look at her baby. It was difficult to assess the impact of Charlotte's feeding skills on the baby's weight, as the baby spent 2 nights per week with respite caregivers, which helped to maintain her weight. Further data were not available as Charlotte's baby was admitted to foster-care because of a range of concerns about Charlotte's lifestyle.

Caroline made some progress during the first two sessions following the baseline observations; however, this was neither consistent during the intervention phase nor maintained during follow-up. It was necessary therefore to introduce a second intervention phase for Caroline. Although Caroline's baby was referred to a paediatrician because of concerns about slow weight gain, Caroline did not accept this as problem. Caroline also had an erratic feeding

pattern for her baby, often feeding the baby outside the project. Staff field note comments indicated that Caroline frequently hurried feeds because she wished to go out with friends. As a result Caroline often refused to wind the baby or feed the entire bottle.

Caroline also had limited interaction with her baby and during 31% of all observations did not talk to or look at the baby. On some occasions Caroline was noted to interact very positively with the baby, while during other observations she was talking on her mobile phone while feeding. Caroline's baby became increasingly difficult to feed, often taking more than thirty minutes to finish a bottle and withdrawn and unresponsive to adult attention. Caroline's baby was admitted to foster care where her weight increased dramatically.

Lee's progress was initially slow and she frequently missed out basic safety steps, including strapping the baby into his seat and checking the temperature of the milk. Consequently, the intervention period was extended. Lee was the only mother in the feeding group who had intellectual disabilities. Like the other mothers who had difficulty with feeding, Lee's interaction with the baby was initially limited. During early observations Lee did not talk to or look at the baby, but instead was watching television. Lee accepted advice to switch the television off during feeding, resulting in an immediate improvement in her interaction with the baby. Lee also acted on advice regarding other aspects of feeding and was able to maintain a maximum score.

## Discussion

A skills based behavioural parent education programme was implemented to increase child care skills with seven young mothers and their babies. Following baseline observations across a range of skills, bathing and feeding were identified as requiring intervention because for seven mothers the scores for these tasks fell below the 80% criterion of successful completion of the task analysis checklist. Feldman (1994) found that parenting skills for basic physical care can improve through behavioural intervention for mothers with intellectual disabilities. The results of this programme confirmed these findings for skills related to bathing the baby. Mothers were able to learn the necessary skills quickly and apply them appropriately.

Results were less defined for feeding the baby. While most mothers were able to learn how to prepare a bottle and feed the baby, only for two of the mothers were these skills maintained and applied appropriately. In addition but for reasons unrelated to the programme, the babies of two of the other mothers who participated in the feeding programme were placed in local authority care before their mothers were able to complete the feeding programme. The mother who had been diagnosed with intellectual disabilities was able to successfully complete the feeding skills programme although she required prolonged training.

Of course, it is difficult to compare results between Feldman's and our work directly because of the difference in the setting and the background of the mothers who participated in these programmes. Mothers who participated in our programme had been referred to a residential unit because of serious concerns about their ability to care for their children. Many of these mothers grew up in care themselves and some had intellectual disabilities. Before being permitted to move into the community with their children they were required to undergo an intensive residential parenting assessment. In contrast, Feldman's participants were older and more than 50% were married. They also lived independently with their children, indicating that child protection issues were less acute than with parents on our programme. The most successful mother in our feeding programme, Lee, had intellectual disabilities and while it took a few extra sessions for her to acquire the skills, once the skills were learned they were successfully maintained by

naturally occurring contingencies, indicating that Lee's difficulties were linked to a skills deficit rather than other issues. Having said this, it is likely that without intervention Lee's skills deficits might have been misread as evidence of inability to parent, possibly resulting in her baby being admitted into care.

Although bathing and feeding may appear to require similar levels of skills, there are some key differences. Bathing the baby is a relatively low demand but highly flexible activity. Bathing usually takes around 5–10 minutes and can easily be arranged around other activities. Mothers can select the time they want to bath their babies and do not necessarily have to do this on a daily basis. The time to bath a baby does not depend on the baby's imminent need; in other words, the bath can wait a while, if something else 'crops up'.

In contrast, feeding a young baby is a high demand and low flexibility activity; it has to happen multiple times per day, it takes quite a long time, up to half an hour or more with young babies, and the baby largely dictates meal times. In addition, some babies are particularly difficult to feed. Babies generally cry when they are hungry and need to be fed. This can place pressure on mothers particularly if the baby's food is not ready when needed and thus feeding is delayed by preparation time. Behaviour analytically speaking, crying is an aversive stimulus and negatively reinforces any parental behaviour that stops the crying.

This negative reinforcement trap led to most mothers becoming dependant on staff prompts to start and then continue feeding their baby until the bottle was empty, rather than taking their prompt from the baby's behaviour. Of course, the fact that staff repeatedly highlighted the steps that were missed also constituted an aversive stimulus and led to some of the mothers becoming increasingly reluctant to engage in observations. Thus staff prompts appeared to act as a negative reinforcer for some of the mothers who had difficulty with the programme and thus simply learnt to avoid staff.

On the other hand, the parent's responsiveness to their child's cries shape the crying behaviour of their babies. If parents only responded when crying is loud and prolonged, as was the case when bottles were not immediately available, it is likely that loud and prolonged crying was reinforced by eventually being fed, which in turn increased pressure on the parent. The reverse is also true, if a parent responded to every cry by feeding the baby, it would become difficult to establish a routine for feeding because it is unclear if the child is crying because he is hungry or for other reasons.

Another key issue with feeding is the fact that many of the naturally occurring potential reinforcers are distal rather than proximal, such as the baby thriving and gaining weight. It became clear that these vulnerable mothers were able to learn the actual skills of making a baby's bottle and feeding the baby, but that more complex contingencies prevented these skills from being applied with the appropriate duration or consistency, in other words, feeding was carried out irregularly and tended to end prematurely. The lack of the development of appropriate feeding routines was clearly linked to other external contingencies that had a more powerful effect on the mothers' behaviour. For example, Caroline had a very limited network of support and any attention from friends took precedence over child care. When friends called she rushed the food preparation and missed essential feeding steps. Going out and meeting friends was a strong reinforcer for behaviours that were not related to the baby.

In fact, this was a pattern across many of the mothers. The mothers with the lowest levels of social support from friends or family had most difficulty with their baby's care. In other words, the presence of friends functioned as a Motivation Operation (Michael, 1993) that altered the reinforcer value of the baby's responses, the vouchers, or staff attention and affected the mothers' child care behaviour.

On the other hand, stress can be a Motivation Operation that impacts negatively on the value of reinforcers and the mothers' overall performance. Stress was a factor for some of the mothers in particular because the first child of two of these mothers had been taken into care because of concerns about neglect. These mothers were acutely aware of the potential negative outcomes of the assessments of their parenting skills for their second baby. The very real concern that their second baby too would be removed clearly altered the value of praise or vouchers as potential reinforcers.

All of the mothers who had difficulty in maintaining criterion levels in the feeding programme fed their babies without talking or making eye contact with them. This contrasted with observations during the bathing programme where all mothers interacted appropriately with their children during bath time. Yet, instead of looking at or talking to their babies during feeding, the mothers watched television or talked to staff, other residents, or on mobile phones to their friends. Therefore these mothers missed the opportunity to receive social reinforcers, for example, smiles from their babies and were unlikely to learn to be sensitive to cues provided by their children during feeding.

In turn of course, the lack of contingent maternal responses, in other words reinforcers, for the baby's cues meant that some of the children eventually ceased to offer cues to their mothers. This was particularly evident with Caroline's baby who became increasingly withdrawn and unresponsive to any adult attention. There was also a risk that mothers would blame or reject their babies because of the association between difficulties with feeding and criticism or stress. Overall, feeding seemed to be a highly stressful experience for these mothers due to concerns raised about their babies' weight gain and staff prompts resulting in avoidance of feeding altogether or feeding babies while out of the project so that feeding could not be observed.

In sum, the child care skills programme effectively taught the skills of bathing and feeding the baby, however, two new issues arouse. First, it became clear that while these mothers now had the skills to engage in the appropriate behaviours they did not adhere to appropriate child care routines. Second, it became apparent that especially during feeding these mothers did not interact with their child; they did not 'read' the babies cues nor did they reinforce their babies' approach and interaction behaviours.

The first of these issues was addressed in the programme that focussed on Child Care Routines (Chapter 7). Mother-child interactions were the focus of the programme described in Chapter 10.

# Child Care Routines

There is no doubt that regularity and routines are very important for child care and child development and that unpredictable environments can be the forerunner to behaviour problems. In behavioural terms, routines are considered a measure of behavioural fluency that goes beyond the ability to engage in the behaviour accurately to being able to engage in the behaviour at the appropriate rate (Lindsley, 1991).

With regard to preventing neglect, routines are particularly important because if parents have good routines it means that child care tasks are carried out in the same or similar way and at predictable times of the day. Routines make child care predictable, reliable, and dependable because they are based on repetition and thus offer opportunities for practicing all sorts of skills for parents and children. Of course, routines are different for each family, some people like to get up early while others enjoy a lie-in, some people eat at set times, while others are more flexible. Regardless of the exact routine in the individual family, the fact is that important things that happen at relatively regular times and are conducted in similar ways ensure that the child is cared for recurrently thus preventing the omission of child care behaviours.

Routines are equally important for parents. They save energy for forward planning, because everyone 'knows' what to do and thus they can prevent conflict, for example, a baby who has a good bedtime routine generally does not fuss when it comes to bedtime. Routines reduce the need for external prompts and encourage young parents to take responsibility for child care, especially if they played a key role in designing the routines. When parents have limited social contacts, having a structured routine means that they have more free time to establish and maintain social contacts.

In order to achieve fluency in child care tasks, parents not only require the skills to perform child care tasks accurately, they also need to be able to perform these tasks at the appropriate rate, which means that the behaviour occurs in a consistent routine appropriate way, at the right time, and at the right frequency. Participants in the feeding and bathing programme learned the necessary skills to complete child care tasks relatively easily and quickly, but some of the participants were unable to perform these new skills reliably both in terms of timing and frequency. This was a problem mainly with regard to feeding the baby, in other words, some of the mothers needed staff prompts to feed their baby, making them prompt – dependent and resentful.

Disorganised routines can have serious consequences for children and cause stress for parents. For example, some mothers in the previous chapter were not prepared in time for feeding. This meant that they had to wash and sterilise bottles, boil the kettle, make up milk formula, and wait for bottles to cool, while their child was crying because they were hungry. In some cases this delayed feeding for up to an hour. On the other hand, when nappies were not changed regularly, the baby developed nappy rash, in some cases their skin was broken and bleeding. This is clearly painful for the child and likely to result in increased crying, which in turn increases pressure on parents. Professionals highlighting these issues can become aversive stimuli, cornering parents in a negative reinforcement trap of avoidance of professional contact.

Self-evidently the cumulative effects of inadequate child care skills and routines as well as avoidance of child care advice and guidance lead to increased risk of child neglect. A baby that is fed later than normal on one occasion would not be classed as neglected but a picture of neglect emerges when a parent is regularly failing to meet the child's needs such as repeatedly missing feeds or failing to bath or change the baby, in other words when there is a consistent pattern omission of child care behaviours.

This programme was developed to address this issue by encouraging parents to design their own routines for the frequency and timing of carrying out child care tasks. Work undertaken aimed to ascertain if parents were able to identify what constitutes a reasonable routine for their child and assess the impact of planning and contracting on routines. Parents were enabled to track their daily patterns of child care and monitor their own progress and were offered positive reinforcement for following routine plans. Parents were encouraged to identify and address other factors that impacted on their routines.

Three mothers and children took part in this programme. Susan had not participated in the bathing and feeding programme because she had reached criterion levels on all child care skills during baseline observations and therefore did not require intervention for managing these skills. Ruby and Caroline both participated in the first programme and their babies were 7 and 3 months old respectively by the time they started the routine programme. Both had the necessary skills for bathing, feeding and other child care tasks, and although they had reached criterion levels in terms of accuracy when carrying out these tasks, had difficulties maintaining these tasks consistently. All three mothers had irregular daily patterns of eating and sleeping themselves.

## Susan

Following the death of her father when she was 12 years old Susan was taken into care and moved through a series of children's homes and foster homes; placements frequently broke down because of Susan's unmanageable behaviour. Susan frequently absconded, was aggressive towards professionals, and misused solvents. She had physically assaulted her mother and was due to appear in court. Susan was 17 years of age when she moved to the project when her baby was 5 days old. At the start of work on routines, the baby was 3 weeks old. Susan was on a Care Order and her baby was on the Child Protection Register under the category of Potential Neglect.

After the birth of the baby Susan received practical and emotional support from her mother. Susan's mother lived 50 miles away from the project and did not drive, however during the initial three weeks she visited Susan three times per week and maintained daily telephone contact. After the first three weeks, her mother's visits became much less frequent, although Susan visited her once per week.

Following a reduction in contact with her mother, Susan's care of her baby became disorganised and erratic. She changed the baby's nappy much less frequently than previously, the baby had developed nappy rash, thrush, and an infected umbilicus, and infrequent bathing of the baby slowed down healing.

Susan often was not prepared in advance of feeds, which resulted in either a delay before the baby was fed or feeding from non-sterilised bottles. Susan spent long periods away from the project, where all the baby care equipment was easily accessible, making it increasingly difficult for her to undertake necessary child care tasks in a planned way. Susan's baby was settled and placid and only cried when she was hungry.

## Ruby

Background information on Ruby was outlined in Chapter 6. While Ruby had learned new child care skills during the first programme, she did not keep to adequate child care routines. The main concerns for her baby were lack of weight gain and extensive nappy rash. There were also concerns that Ruby's baby was often put down for more sleeps than he needed. Staff had frequently found the baby in his cot awake, particularly on days when Ruby appeared to be under pressure. On other occasions the baby slept for very long periods during the day. Staff suspected that Ruby was using over-the-counter teething pain medication to mildly sedate the baby and get him over to sleep more than necessary.

Ruby had difficulty remaining in her accommodation alone with the baby and often spent time with staff or other residents away from her flat, which prevented her from carrying out child care tasks. Ruby's baby presented as a quiet settled baby.

## Caroline

Caroline had taken part in the bathing and feeding programme and was able to learn the necessary child care skills, but had no regular child care routines, partly due to the fact that she spent lengthy periods away from the project. Caroline's baby was not gaining weight at the expected rate and prior to taking part in the routine programme she had been asked to keep a record of feeding times and durations. However, Caroline rarely filled in her feeding record and often failed to administer prescribed medication. Caroline had frequent visitors to her accommodation, which disrupted planned routines. Informal observations and field notes showed that Caroline was able to complete tasks, when she was supervised but failed to do so without staff presence.

## Materials

The identification of individual priorities for this programme was based on informal observations by staff who, together with the mothers, identified feeding, bathing, play, nappy changing, preparing for feeds, and sleep routines as key child care tasks that needed to be completed at regular intervals throughout the day. Subsequently, all three mothers completed a daily diary to identify the normal times when these tasks were completed and the usual times when the babies slept, so that a routine could be developed around the baby's normal sleeping and waking patterns. Examples of materials used are in Practice Tool 2.

Individualised behavioural contracts were developed to identify the minimum frequency and latest time-of-day for completion for each task. Tasks were planned around the babies' natural routines and mothers were required to record task completion during baseline and intervention on individualised charts developed for this programme. New tasks were added to the contract when previous targets were reached and time spent away from the project was recorded to assess the impact this had on each mother's ability to follow routines.

Target behaviours differed for each mother. Susan's target behaviours were frequency and timing of preparing for feeds, feeding, changing nappies, and bathing the baby. Susan played and interacted with her baby appropriately and therefore intervention for interaction was not required.

Safeguarding priorities dictated the sequence in which behaviours were targeted for example, Susan frequently did not feed her baby because bottles had not been sterilised in advance. Therefore, in the behavioural contract Susan agreed that bottles were to be sterilised by 12 noon every day. She agreed to give her baby the first bottle no later than 10 a.m. and subsequently give the baby a bottle at 3–4 hourly intervals throughout the day.

Susan did not change the baby's nappy frequently enough and her baby suffered from severe nappy rash and thrush. Consequently nappy changing was identified as the next target behaviour. Susan agreed to change nappies every three hours, using at least five fresh nappies per day. On a number of occasions Susan had not bathed the baby for three days therefore she agreed to bath the baby each morning by 11 a.m. and wash the baby's face and bottom (colloquially referred to as 'top and tail') each evening before 10 p.m.

Target behaviours for Ruby were frequency and timing of her baby's feeding, bathing, nappy changing, sleeping, and play. Feeding was targeted first, because Ruby's baby was considered low-weight. Ruby agreed to feed her baby age appropriately with bottles and solids with no more than 4 hours interval between feeding and a minimum of 4 meals per day. Ruby preferred to bath her baby in the evening. She agreed to bath her baby daily by 7 p.m. and to 'top and tail' the baby by 10 a.m. each day. Ruby agreed to change the baby's nappy at least every 4 hours when the baby was awake with a minimum of 4 nappy changes per day. Initially the agreed sleep routine for Ruby's baby was to allow two half-hour naps during the day, however this proved to be too short and 2 weeks into the intervention this was adjusted to 45 minutes. Ruby also agreed to have the baby settled for the night between 7.30 p.m. and 8 p.m. Ruby agreed to play with her baby, defined as any positive face to face interaction other than completing child care tasks, 4 times per day for at least 10 minutes each time.

Caroline had no regular child care routines, partly due to spending lengthy periods away from the project. Caroline's baby was not gaining weight at the expected rate and although Caroline was to keep a record of the number of bottles she fed the baby, to explore the reasons for the low weight, she rarely filled in her feeding record and often failed to administer prescribed medication. Caroline frequently had visitors to her home, which seriously disrupted child care routines. The initial focus of the programme was on carrying out child care tasks at a specific time of day and to ensure that she completed tasks. Caroline was closely supervised during set times. Her programme procedure was therefore somewhat different from the other two mothers' and will be reported in part 2 of the routine programme.

## Part 1

### Procedure

A member of staff met with Susan and Ruby regularly to review progress against agreed timing and frequency targets for specific child care behaviour. A token economy system using vouchers and social praise from staff were used for both mothers as reinforcers for completed child care routines and an additional voucher was earned for completing the recording sheet. To ensure that routines did not become overly rigid and remained sensitive to the babies' needs, targets were set at 80% of correct completion of routines. Charts were reviewed frequently with the mother. Mothers continued to keep a record of time spent away from the project, to analyse how this impacted on child care.

A multiple baseline across behaviours was used; however, in some cases the urgency of child care tasks did not allow for stabilising baseline measures. Measures were taken of the percentage of the tasks that were completed within the time frame set by each mother. This was calculated as percentage correct on a daily basis, as follows:

$$\frac{\text{Number of times task was completed within the agreed time} \times 100}{\text{Maximum possible score for that task}}$$

Inter-observer agreement was calculated between mothers' own recordings and staff observations. Staff observed between 3–4 feeding sessions per day for each mother. Inter-observer agreement was calculated as follows:

$$\frac{\text{Number of agreements} \times 100}{\text{Total number of feeds}}$$

The inter-observer agreement was 97% for Susan. On the few occasions on which staff recording did not match with Susan's, this was due to the fact that Susan started feeding before staff come into the flat for observation, for example, she began to feed the baby at 4.50 p.m. and therefore recorded that feeding happened between 4–5 o'clock box, whereas when staff came in at 5 p.m. for the observation session, they observed the end of feeding at 5.10 p.m. and recorded feeding happened at 5–6 o'clock. The inter-observer agreement for Ruby for feeding was slightly lower at 87%, because Ruby forgot to record on a number of occasions.

Follow-up data were not available because Susan had stopped recording before all behaviours had been targeted and Ruby stopped recording before all behaviours stabilised.

## Results

Although there had been concerns about Susan's ability to feed her baby frequently enough and at the right time, this was not reflected during

baseline recordings. Susan scored at or above the 80% criterion level for the first 6 days of baseline, however after that, scores dropped as low as 33% reflecting that the baby experienced long delays between feeds. During the intervention phase the average feeding score was 84%; yet, on four occasions Susan did not meet criterion levels, the lowest score was 66%. Susan prepared bottles by the planned time and maintained this during 70% of the intervention phase.

Some initial improvement occurred in the frequency of nappy changing during baseline; however, this was not maintained and led to severe nappy rash. There was a marked improvement initially during the first 6 days of the intervention phase; however, this improvement was not maintained and during the following 3 days nappy changing became very infrequent. Susan stopped recording when she was bathing the baby before the intervention was implemented. Although Susan had agreed in the contract to bath and 'top and tail' the baby on a daily basis, baseline recordings reflect an 8 day period when the baby was not bathed at all and washed only 5 times.

Casual observations indicated that Susan did not get up in the mornings until well after 10 a.m. At the same time, the baby began to sleep through the night, which meant that not only did baby miss being fed during the night but also missed the first feed in the morning. Moreover, the baby's nappy was not changed for lengthy periods and instead of caring for her baby, Susan spent long periods of time on the phone to friends, in other residents' flats, and talking to visitors. Changing, feeding, and safety were severely disrupted by these activities, for example, on one occasion Susan did not respond to the baby when she choked. After 28 days as Susan had continued difficulties with managing most child care tasks, to the extent that the baby had recurring diarrhoea due to poor hygiene, the baby was removed from Susan's care on an Emergency Protection Order.

For Ruby, initial plans to target behaviours individually in sequence were adjusted because of the urgency of establishing adequate routines for child care tasks. Target routines were introduced for two child care behaviours at a time. As a result of self-monitoring alone, Ruby's feeding routine improved during the baseline. Shortly after intervention began, respite child minding was introduced for 2 days per week for 4 hours which resulted in the interval between feeding increasing for Ruby's feeding routine. In fact, there were fluctuations in the frequency of feeding even on days when the baby attended the child minder and Ruby was responsible for only two feeds. Ruby often claimed that her baby refused to eat, although he ate well when fed by workers. Feeding her baby seemed to have become an aversive activity for Ruby; she tended to feed the baby too quickly and at times the food was very dry and she did not provide a drink for the baby.

The bathing intervention began at the same time as the feeding intervention because frequency of bathing during baseline was very low – the baby was bathed only once per week. Bathing increased immediately after the voucher scheme was introduced. Ruby bathed and washed her baby daily for the following 13 days, only missing his bath on one occasion. After 21 days, Ruby changed the target of bathing to alternate days and consequently a decrease in the frequency of bathing was recorded during the last week of intervention.

The voucher scheme was then introduced for routines related to nappy changing and sleeping concurrently. Since the baby had eczema and nappy rash, the target behaviour was for Ruby to change the baby's nappy 4 times per day, when he was awake. Recordings of 100% reflect 4 or more nappy changes, 75% represents 3 nappy changes, and 50% represents 2 nappy changes. Although there was some improvement in the rate of nappy changing, on 2 occasions during intervention the baby's nappy was changed only twice during the course of the whole day.

The relatively high frequency with which Ruby put her baby in his cot for daytime naps limited the opportunities for social interaction and stimulation. The baby was healthy and there was no physical reason for him to require additional sleep. At baseline, the target for frequency and duration of naps was exceeded frequently, for example, Ruby put the baby in the cot for a daytime sleep after breakfast, when the baby had been awake for less than one hour. At other times when he woke during the day, she fed him quickly and put him back into his cot and the baby was frequently observed awake in the cot, at times when Ruby reported that he was sleeping. This pattern improved slightly during intervention, however on three of the intervention days Ruby still exceeded target frequencies of putting the baby in his cot. This coincided with Ruby having difficulties in her relationships with staff and other residents in the project. On the other hand, there were several occasions when the baby had less

sleep than planned because Ruby had other residents visiting her flat making it difficult for her to settle the baby.

Frequency of interaction and play improved following baseline recording for the first week of intervention, however during the last week it became inconsistent. Twice during the last week Ruby recorded that she had only spent one 10-minute session playing with her son all day and on one day she did not play with him at all. These results reflected concerns about the limited interaction between Ruby and her son. When this was discussed with Ruby she did not accept the suggestion that her baby would benefit from an increase in interaction with her but instead stated that he seemed to prefer to lie alone on the floor.

Ruby recorded her child care routines for 37 days and then refused further recording stating that she was 'too busy'. Ruby had collected a number of vouchers during the period of recording and used these to obtain a large toy for her son. Recording stopped following the acquisition of the toy, in other words, the other items on the reinforcer menu did not actually function as reinforcers for continued programme adherence. Despite efforts to find suitable reinforcers, this was not possible at the time and consequently Ruby disengaged from the programme.

Although there were some improvements in the frequency of Ruby carrying out child care tasks during intervention, this was not consistent. Progress was affected mostly by Ruby's need for social contact, mainly with other residents in the project. Clearly social contact functions as a very strong reinforcer for behaviours that were incompatible with child care routines. In addition, Ruby had on-going contact with a former partner, who assaulted her during the second week of the feeding intervention phase. This had a negative impact on all areas of Ruby's child care. Ruby avoided attempts to discuss her progress in maintaining routines, frequently changing the subject or becoming tearful. Eventually, the programme was discontinued.

## Discussion

Child care routines are an important aspect of child care in general and an assessment of routines gives a clear overall picture of the quality of care that a child receives on a daily basis. Results for both mothers showed some, yet inconsistent improvements in their ability to adhere to basic routines for child care tasks. Both mothers were able to plan a routine, but were unable to follow their plans consistently. The use of contracts and self-recording had some initial impact on parental behaviour, however the introduction of vouchers had a limited short-term effect.

It is possible that routines were disrupted because reinforcers were not available until recording was reviewed and data were transcribed. However, delay of reinforcement is a phenomenon that occurs even in terms of naturally occurring reinforcers; most of the behaviours included in child care routines are subject to delayed consequences. Feeding, for example, leads to weight gain, but this is not evident until the baby is weighed at the baby clinic many days after the actual feeding behaviour has occurred. Infrequent nappy changing causes nappy rash, but this is not evident for quite a number of days. Natural reinforcers, such as the child's immediate comfort and wellbeing evidently did not act as a reinforcer for the parents in this programme and consequently emerged as important focus for further intervention which is addressed in Chapter 10.

Ultimately, it was not possible to identify causal relations between intervention and behaviour change due to the fact that, for safeguarding reasons, it was not possible to delay intervention until baseline data were stable. In addition, despite the fact that staff monitoring was in place, parental self-monitoring included the risk of inaccurate recording. This was the case for bathing more so than feeding, because project staff were frequently present during mealtimes. Having said this, the high level of accuracy of recordings for feeding by both mothers suggested that their recordings may have been accurate also in other areas, particularly as both mothers' records indicated where progress was not maintained.

Evidently, this programme was heavily disrupted by competing contingencies. On one hand, these mothers completed their own recordings to avoid staff contact, in other words, the programme was in part affected by the negative reinforcement trap described earlier and consequently, the routine charts became conditioned aversive stimuli and both mothers ultimately stopped recording. On the other hand, these mothers undertook tasks only as long as the staff person was present, thus becoming prompt dependent.

In addition and due to the social isolation of these mothers, the other main factor that impacted on routines for both parents was their need for social contact, which took priority over child care tasks. Both mothers spent long periods of time away from their flats or with other residents in their accommodation, thus accessing immediate social reinforcers for alternative non-child care related behaviours. The second part of the programme addressing routines explored the effect of applying immediate reinforcers to child care routines.

## Part 2

## Caroline

Caroline's background details were described earlier. She spent long periods of time way from her accommodation or had visitors in her flat and consequently her baby did not gain weight. Furthermore, Caroline did not complete her recording sheets or administer the baby's medication regularly. In order to help Caroline establish a child care routine, the programme was individually tailored to meet her needs; as such the completion of child care tasks was targeted to take place during a particular time of the day rather than at specific frequencies or rate.

### Procedure

Target routines for Caroline included preparing bottles, giving prescribed medication to the baby, feeding the baby, completing the feeding chart, bathing the baby, settling the baby for the night, and tidying the flat. Caroline agreed to contract that all child care tasks would be completed between 7 p.m. to 9 p.m. She was included in the design of the monitoring chart and agreed to complete it on a daily basis. The chart covered Sunday to Friday because the baby was in respite care from Saturday morning until Sunday night.

Caroline agreed that she would discourage visitors during the time specified for task completion. Targets for accuracy of task completion were gradually increased from 60% to 70% to 80%. To ensure safeguarding the child throughout the intervention, staff completed any tasks that had not been completed by Caroline.

In addition to the voucher scheme, prompts and help with child care routines were available initially each evening for 2 hours (from 7 p.m. to

9 p.m.). Prompts and help with child care routines included for example, staff holding the baby to allow Caroline to complete other tasks, such as preparing the bottle. The duration of staff availability for help with child care behaviours was faded once target behaviours were stable; during the first week staff were available for 2 hours; in the second week staff were present and help and prompts were available for 30 minutes, then staff left the flat for 30 minutes to allow Caroline to complete the child care tasks on her own, then staff returned for further 30 minutes to offer help and prompts where necessary. During the third week staff help and prompts were faded further and available for 15 minutes at the beginning and a further 15 minutes at end of the 2-hour time window that was set for child care task completion. Further fading of staff support meant that subsequently, there were random checks during the 2-hour period to ensure that Caroline was completing child care tasks. Finally, checks were completed only at the end of each 2-hour period and completed tasks were recorded on Caroline's Evening Routine Chart. Vouchers and verbal praise were given as reinforcer for completed steps on a daily basis.

Target behaviours were measures in percent correct of the steps on the routine plan completed by the planned time without prompts from staff. Percent correct was calculated as follows

$$\frac{\text{Number of steps completed by}}{\text{agreed time} \times 100}$$
$$\frac{}{\text{Total number of required steps}}$$

A changing criterion design was used to monitor effectiveness of the programme. The weekly target criterion was raised based on the data recorded in the previous week; up to a maximum of 80% correct task completion. The maximum was set at 80% to allow some flexibility, for example, if the baby refused a feed or was unsettled. The use of a changing criterion design meant that target criterion were slowly increased, which ensured that there were frequent opportunities for positive reinforcement during the intervention.

## Results

During baseline Caroline completed few of the routine tasks and was prompted frequently. Caroline had visitors in her flat during this time distracting her from completion of child care tasks. There was a marked improvement in the number of tasks completed at the beginning of the intervention, in other words, when the contract was agreed about completion of child care routines, visitors were discouraged, and continuous prompting was available, for example, staff reminding Caroline about giving medication to the baby etc. Initially, on-going encouragement was required for Caroline to stay on task. During the first week, the only step missed was completion of the feeding chart. Once a prompt was given for Caroline to complete this chart, she completed it over the following two weeks (Figure 7.1).

During the second and third week of intervention Caroline met or surpassed rising criterion levels with the exception of one day when she did not complete any child care tasks on time, except for putting the baby to bed on time. This was due to visitors calling at the flat.

During weeks 4 and 5 of intervention, safeguarding concerns about Caroline's child care meant that staff remained present during most of the routine. Scores decreased dramatically over the final 8 recordings because Caroline returned late to the flat and therefore engaged in child care tasks later than planned; she had to be prompted to undertake all tasks and was frequently in other residents' flats or had visitors in her accommodation. Eventually the baby was taken into hospital due to feeding difficulties and on discharge from hospital remained in Caroline's care for only one week. During this week Caroline refused to undertake any further work on routines and due to the level of concern about the quality of care provided, the baby was taken into foster care.

## Discussion

Although progress of child care task completion was not maintained for Caroline, Part 2 of this programme showed a steadier progress than Part 1. Focussing child care routines on a specific time of day meant that there was more time for the mother to engage in other activities and thus child care routines became less daunting. In Caroline's case clearly there was the need for very high levels of staff support and prompting and reinforcer delivery (verbal praise) initially was given immediately after each completion of a child care task. Later on, when verbal praise was used intermittently things began to 'fall apart'.

Caroline's charts were kept in the project office so other members of staff could monitor her progress and offer additional praise. Charting

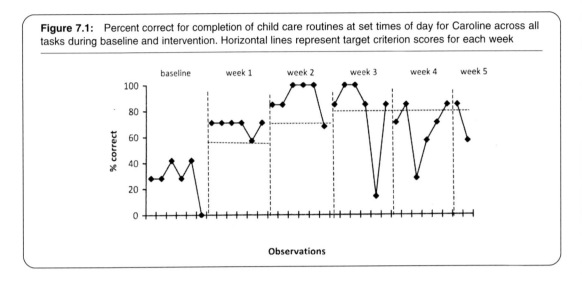

**Figure 7.1:** Percent correct for completion of child care routines at set times of day for Caroline across all tasks during baseline and intervention. Horizontal lines represent target criterion scores for each week

Caroline's progress was simpler than Susan's and Ruby's in Part 1 and Caroline was able to clearly understand her charts. Of course, there were also drawbacks to implementing child care routines during set periods of time as this programme failed to address routines at other times of the day and thus could have resulted in the child not receiving adequate care outside the structured routine times. In Caroline's case this was prevented by additional support from staff and foster care.

## General discussion

This programme showed that young vulnerable mothers were able to identify the timing and frequency of each child care task and carry out all necessary tasks as planned. However, the programme also identified a number of issues that impeded long-term success for some mothers and their babies. Clearly, the precursor of any child care routine programme is to ensure that the parent has the necessary skills. Parent education and training to achieve accurate performance of each child care task was outlined in the feeding and bathing programme described in the previous chapter. This programme offered an insight into the actual procedures of how to establish reliable child care routines, in other words, to ensure that parents carry out necessary child care skill at the appropriate rate and level and at the right time. In behaviour analysis the term fluency is used for this process. For prevention of neglect it is important that parents achieve fluency in child

care tasks and that this fluency is maintained in the long-term.

While the mothers agreed to and were able to learn and carry out child care routines initially, the long-term maintenance of these behaviours was a problem. Most of the mothers who took part in the routine programme were unable to sustain progress when competing contingencies were present. In the case of these young mothers competing contingencies came in the form of social contact with peers.

The mothers in the project had low levels of social support beyond formal supports; therefore this isolation functioned as a Motivational Operation which resulted in social contact becoming a very powerful reinforcer. Many of their social contacts resented mothers being unavailable because of child care demands and, functionally speaking, offered reinforcers for many behaviours that were incompatible with child care routines, such as going out for a drink, going shopping, having a party. For example, Susan's child care routines during the initial weeks in the project were of a good standard. This was the case while she received positive reinforcers for child care behaviours on a regular basis from her mother. In addition, her mother undertook some of the child care tasks so she also had the opportunity for observational learning in relation to child care. This suggested that social contacts that also offer reinforcers for appropriate child care can improve standards of child care. The problem was that most of the mothers' friends were not interested in the babies and consequently did not reinforce child care routines.

Generally, the child's wellbeing provides sufficient positive reinforcers for child care behaviours and the potential discomfort of the child acts as negative reinforcer. However this was not the case for most of the socially isolated mothers in the project. They generally were not sensitive to the child's needs and thus their wellbeing did not function to reinforce child care behaviours. Mattaini & Thyer (1996) suggested that interventions that ensure that the child's wellbeing becomes an effective reinforcer for child care are central to improving outcomes in cases of neglect.

Increasing positive interactions with the child and making parents more aware of the positive effect they can have on their child's behaviour will be explored further in the Parent Child Interaction Programme described in Chapter 10. Before that, we will address two other issues that arose during the earlier programmes; first, flats were not kept 'child safe' in terms of actual dangers, such as kitchen knives and bleach being accessible to toddlers and second, there was a risk of infection for babies due to the fact that the flats were not kept clean and hygienic. Therefore, the following two programmes will address Home Safety and Home Hygiene.

# CHAPTER 8

# Home Safety

Unsafe home environments can result in injury or death of a child. In fact, the most common causes of death in children under five years of age are drowning, scalding, poisoning, and fires that happen in the home when a carer is not present at the critical moment to safeguard the child. Accidents that happen in families where children are usually well supervised and parents are careful about keeping potential hazards out of child's reach are usually not considered neglect in terms of child safeguarding legislation. However, an unsafe home environment where hazards, such as knives and other sharp instruments, cleaning products, or open fires are accessible is a dangerous place for the unsupervised child and can be an indicator of neglect.

Accidents in the home are most common for children aged one to two years of age, who live in families with more than one sibling, especially if parents are young, parenting alone and lack social supports. Living rooms are the most common place for accidents; however bedrooms, kitchens and stairs are also hazardous places. Difficulties increase for parents who have few social contacts as this often means there is no one else who can help care for their child to allow them to complete everyday household or child care tasks, for example they may have to supervise an active toddler or preschool child while cooking or doing housework.

The Home Safety Programme focussed on reducing hazards in the home by educating parents about potential risks and teaching them how to remove dangers to the child by adjustments in the home environment. In order to ensure generalisation and maintenance of parental behaviour changes the young mothers were involved in identifying dangers and potentially hazardous outcomes for children. The programme focussed on mothers taking responsibility for identifying and removing hazards thereby creating a safe home environment for their children. The materials and procedure used for the Home Safety Programme can be found in Practice Tool 3.

The programme also included parent education with regard to the developmental needs of the child, especially in terms of the level of supervision required for young babies and toddlers. Developmental issues were important because some young parents overestimated the ability of their children to keep themselves out of danger or underestimated the child's ability to get into dangerous situations. For example, the assumption that a 10 month old baby would 'know' not to crawl close up to the open fire or that a 2 year old toddler would not climb on a chair to reach bleach on the kitchen table.

The level of supervision required for a child is difficult to quantify. The developmental level of the child dictates how much supervision is needed and this changes on a near daily basis as the child learns new skills. At times parents need to fully supervise their children, for example when bathing a young baby, while at other times supervision from the 'corner of your eye' suffices, such as for 3–4 year old children who play with their toys on the living room floor.

Modifying the environment to reduce hazards in the home and therefore reducing the level of supervision necessary allows children more freedom to explore and learn. Risk taking is a normal part of child development and one way that children learn about their environments. Undoubtedly, unsafe home environments affect child development and the parent-child relationship, as children are exposed to high rates of instruction, such as 'be careful', 'don't do that'. A safer home decreases aversive control and avoids preventable accidents.

The Home Safety Programme was conducted in two parts. The first part focused on developing the Home Safety Checklist and the second part centred on fine-tuning and individually tailoring the categories the Home Safety Checklist.

## Part 1

### Judy

Judy, 19 years of age and her 18 month-old daughter were referred to the project because of concerns about the potential neglect of the baby, mainly related to the levels of hygiene and safety when Judy was living in her own home. Judy's accommodation in the project was often untidy and posed a number of potential dangers for her daughter.

Judy was living with her parents prior to admission to the project, although previously she had lived independently with her daughter for a short time. Judy had a supportive relationship with her parents but professionals involved with the family were concerned also about standards of safety and hygiene in her parents' home. Judy had a very positive relationship with her daughter and was able to undertake all necessary child care tasks. She engaged in appropriate child care routines, however, needed to learn basic home management skills.

Judy's daughter was a very lively child who was steady on her feet but not yet climbing onto furniture. The child's name was on the child protection register under the category of potential neglect.

## Lynne

Lynne was 17 years old and initially had wanted to put her baby daughter up for adoption. The baby was cared for in a foster home and Lynne had very little contact with her daughter, who was 8 months old when they moved to the project to give Lynne the opportunity to care for her daughter.

Lynne herself grew up in foster care because of neglect by her own parents and had lost touch with her natural family. The foster placement had broken down and Lynne had no contact with her foster family. Lynne's overall child care was of a good standard, however as her daughter became increasingly mobile it was evident that Lynne often underestimated potential risks to her daughter. Lynne's daughter was one year old at the time of the programme and had just begun to walk.

## *Materials*

The Home Safety Checklist was devised to identify hazards within the flats (see Practice Tool 3) and was loosely based on the Home Accident Prevention Inventory (HAPI) (Tertinger, Greene, & Lutzker, 1984). However, many hazards identified in the HAPI programme did not apply

to families living in temporary accommodation, for example, parents in the project did not store items such as paint and did not have open fires. Given that the project was a care provider, the safety of all equipment, including cots or electrical equipment, was the responsibility of the project management team who undertook regular inspections to ensure that the items in each flat met safety standards. To ensure applicability to the setting, the Home Safety Checklist was therefore individually tailored for each mother-child dyad and their specific accommodation.

In the Home Safety Checklist, 'dangers' were divided into seven general categories including:

(a) supervision and falls
(b) hygiene
(c) choking
(d) ingestion
(e) fire & burns
(f) electric shocks
(g) suffocation.

Each category was divided into further subcategories to reflect the most common causes of serious or fatal accidents of children in the home as identified by staff observations of individual parent's behaviour, staff experience with previous residents, and information from the Child Accident Prevention Trust (1989). On the recording sheet 'dangers' were classed as present only if a child had access to them and were classed as not present if they were out of the child's reach or in a locked cupboard.

Mothers were asked to complete a sheet listing the 'dangers' that had been identified. During the initial assessment all mothers listed the possible consequences of each hazard for the child, and identified necessary steps to remove or fix the danger. This ensured that the programme was based on the developmental level of the individual child and encouraged each mother to identify dangers as they could affect her child, rather than removing dangers because they had been instructed to do so.

## *Procedure*

A number of members of staff were trained in the use of the home safety assessments. Training involved an explanation of the dangers that were included on the sheet and a trial observation in one of the flats that had been specially arranged to ensure that hazards were present in all categories. Following training staff completed a written test. Scores obtained ranged from 85% to 100% correct. Interobserver agreement (IOA) was calculated using the following formula:

$$\frac{\text{Number of Agreements} \times 100}{\text{Number of Agreements} + \text{Number of Disagreements}}$$

During the intervention, IOA scores across all categories averaged 88% and ranged from 71% to 100%.

In order to individualise assessment to the level of danger each child had access to, the physical height of the standing child (to eye level) and their reach, were measured with a tape measure. The child's ability to climb was also assessed. Dangers that were placed higher than the child's ability to climb or reach were not included in the assessment of accessible dangers.

The procedure was explained to each mother and the importance of making homes safe for children was outlined. Observations were undertaken in each mother's flat. Each room was assessed by walking through once in a clockwise direction, recording each danger present on the checklist. Small objects that could potentially choke a child were checked in a 'choke tube', any object that fitted entirely within the tube was classed as a choking hazard. The tape measure was used to measure if potentially harmful objects were within the child's reach.

Intervention consisted of the following:

1. Mothers accompanied the observer when completing the checklist and were encouraged to identify any dangers described on the sheet and tell the observer how this could be remedied. If mothers were unable to identify any hazards, a member of staff explained why something was considered dangerous and ways of removing or fixing the danger.
2. Mothers had a list of dangers to fix or remove before the next observation and were asked to complete a list, outlining potential consequences for their child, and how risks could be removed.
3. A contract was drawn up agreeing tasks to be undertaken by the mother and the observer; setting target scores for the following week, and the agreed reinforcer if targets were met.
4. Necessary safety equipment was recorded, including socket guards, safety gates and high shelves.

5. Each mother identified a final reinforcer for completion of the programme individually. Both were relatively expensive in terms of resources and staff time:
   (a) Lynne wanted a meal cooked by a member of staff.
   (b) Judy requested a night out with a member of staff.

The total number of dangers present and the number of dangers in each category were recorded.

## Results

A changing criterion single-system research design was used with both mothers. Each week the gradually reducing criterion scores were negotiated with each mother, based on the score obtained on the previous observation. Behavioural contracts were adjusted accordingly.

Given baseline observations of 27 dangers in Judy's flat, the criterion scores at the start of her intervention were set at 13. Judy was able to undercut the initial criterion level and consequently the criterion was lowered to 5 for subsequent observations. Judy was able to meet this criterion on one occasion but not on the second observation.

Judy reached criterion scores for almost all dangers during intervention and was able to maintain this for 3 observations. The improvement was particularly noticeable for 'hygiene' where a relatively high baseline score was reduced almost immediately. For 'electrical shock' the first observation during intervention did not meet criterion levels, while the following 2 observations showed an improvement. With regard to 'ingestion' the criterion was not reached during intervention. In fact, the number of ingestion hazards present in the flat during the third intervention observation exceeded the baseline observation.

The main category where dangers were present was 'ingestion' and consisted of cosmetics, shampoos and medicines that were within her child's reach in the bathroom. Judy had identified the potential consequences of her child swallowing any of these items and included 'keeping them out of reach' in her plan for reducing dangers, but had not done this. Follow-up data were not available as Judy moved into her own house and further observations were

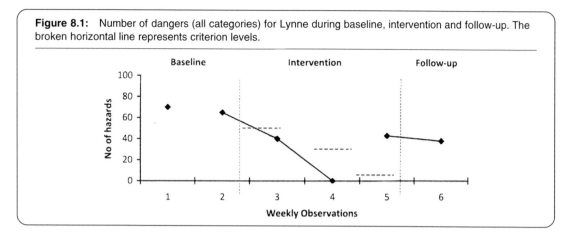

**Figure 8.1:**  Number of dangers (all categories) for Lynne during baseline, intervention and follow-up. The broken horizontal line represents criterion levels.

not feasible due to the distance from the project. However family support services reported that the improvement in overall standards in the home was maintained in the community and Judy's child's name was removed from the child protection register soon after discharge from the project.

Following baseline assessment, in which Lynne scored 70+ dangers in her flat and her weekly target criterion was set initially at 50 and then reduced to 30 and then 5 combined hazards. As shown in Figure 8.1 Lynne did not reach criterion scores during the first few observations, however, she did remove all dangers prior to the fourth observation. Lynne moved into the community after the fourth observation and follow-up observations were undertaken in her new home.

Across categories of dangers the highest scores were in the categories 'supervision' because a large number of ornamental, decorative items and sharp objects were within the reach of her child. The category of 'ingestion' was relatively high due to medication and cosmetics that were within the reach of the child. While reductions in the overall number of hazards were not maintained at follow-up this was largely due to the fact that follow-up data were taken in the new flat in the community where there were no 'child proof areas'; there was no bathroom cabinet, lockable cupboard, or high shelves in the living room. As Lynne had moved to privately rented accommodation she needed her landlord's permission to make any alterations. However, as a result of the intervention, she was able to identify all dangers that were present and address this with the landlord.

## Discussion

The Home Safety Intervention was effective in raising each mother's awareness of potential dangers and enabling the mothers to keep their homes safer, thus potentially preventing injury to their child. However, merely counting individual items did not give a realistic picture of the levels of safety in each of the flats. Although both mothers succeeded in reducing the numbers of dangers present in their homes, this was not fully reflected in frequency results because counting each item as a separate hazard gave an inflated sense of how unsafe their homes really were. For example, the increase in the number of hazards following intervention for both mothers was caused by cosmetics being within reach in the bathroom, although both mothers had made significant progress in reducing hazards in other rooms in their homes.

Very young children are rarely left alone in the bathroom and are much more likely to experience accidents in more commonly used areas like living rooms. Since living rooms were kept increasingly free of hazards, the relatively high average hazard score in some of the categories was not a true reflection of risks to the children. Qualitative feedback from both mothers indicated that they found the procedure useful.

In order to reflect areas of the home where accidents are most likely to happen, Part 2 of this programme reported on dangers categorised according to the rooms in which they occurred. The procedure was also adapted with regard to a number of other issues; for example, the scoring method. In Part 1 scoring was based on a frequency count of the total number of dangers and therefore a high score indicated a high number of dangers. The mothers considered this confusing because in assessment instruments used in previous programmes a high score had indicated progress. Mothers also suggested that counting the total number of dangers in each category, for example, counting the total numbers of sharp knives, gave unrealistic scores. They pointed out that a child could just as easily be injured if they had access to one knife, as opposed to several.

## Part 2

## Karen

Karen was 20 years of age when she moved to the project with her two sons aged 1 and 2 years of age. Karen had intellectual disabilities and problems with literacy and was on anti-depressant medication. Karen's older child was very active and big for his age. He was diagnosed with global developmental delay and behaviour problems. In contrast, the younger child presented as a quieter, less demanding child.

Prior to her move to the project, Karen was living in a hostel and was in a violent relationship with a partner. Following the break-up of this relationship, concern was raised about the quality of care that Karen was able to provide for the children on her own. In particular, Karen had difficulty managing her eldest son's behaviour and daily routines, and hygiene and safety standards in the home were low. Karen had little understanding of the children's developmental levels, for example, her eldest son was nearly 3 years of age and was not toilet trained. Karen often underestimated her children's ability, for example, although she had previously seen her older child playing with the lock of the flat door, she took no precautions to prevent him from locking himself in or out the flat on his own. In addition, while Karen was unable to carry out more than one task at a time, she had problems with supervising the children, for example, while she was using the telephone. Consequently, both children's names were on the Child Protection Register under the category of potential neglect.

Karen was selected for the Home Safety Programme because both children had been exposed to dangerous situations that could have been avoided. In fact, her younger son had fractured his arm twice when he fell off furniture on which he was climbing while unsupervised and her older son was nearly hit by a car while he was outside on a walk. Karen had literacy problems and therefore staff observers read out materials to her.

## Cathleen

Cathleen was 19 years of age when she moved to the project with her two sons who were aged 1 and 3 years at that time. Before admission Cathleen's children had been in foster care due to domestic violence from a former partner, Cathleen's drug and alcohol misuse, contact with convicted sex offenders, and low standards of care for the children. Cathleen was diagnosed with depression and was on prescribed medication.

Cathleen's older son was a very articulate child, who was advanced in all areas of development, while the younger child was passive compared to his brother and demanded very little attention from his mother or other adults. Both children were on Care Orders and registered on the Child Protection Register under the category of potential neglect.

Since admission Catherine had failed to attend the children's medical appointments, had not administered prescribed medication, and had placed the baby in his cot for long periods of time. She did not provide adequate play or stimulation for the children and consequently they became increasingly difficult to manage. The older son used offensive languages and kicked his mother. Cathleen believed that the younger child rejected her because he did not want to be cuddled by her, although both children were affectionate, responsive, and easily engaged with project staff.

While Cathleen's depression appeared to improve as her placement progressed and she became more outgoing with staff and other residents, her behaviour towards the children did not change; their diets continued to be poor, their routines fitted around Cathleen's activities, and because Cathleen spent more and more time with other residents she interacted progressively less with the children. Cathleen took part in the Home Safety Programme because a number of avoidable accidents had resulted in injuries and bruises to the children.

## *Materials*

The Home Safety Checklist developed in Part 1 was adapted and individualised and a small number of additional items were identified. The scoring system was changed to record the absence, rather than the presence, of hazards in each room. A percentage score for each room was calculated by dividing the total score obtained by the maximum possible score for that area, multiplied by 100. When hazards were present a score of zero was given, the actual number of hazards did not affect the score.

The observation procedure remained the same as in Part 1. In both families the physical measures of height and reach were taken of the taller child to ascertain which objects would be within reach for all children in a family.

## Procedure

A multiple baseline across settings design was combined with a changing criterion design. On a weekly basis criterion levels were increased by 10% of the scores reached for the previous week. Observations were conducted in each room of each family's flat.

Intervention remained the same as in Part 1, in other words, both mothers were awarded vouchers for reaching criterion levels and vouchers then were used to 'buy' from an individual list of preferred reinforcer items. Safety scores were recorded for each room separately. Rooms with a safety score below 80% during baseline were selected for intervention. Rooms where families spent most of their time and thus accidental injury was more likely to happen, in other words, kitchens and living rooms were targeted first. Intervention continued until a safety score of 90% or above was achieved over three observations.

## Results

Karen's scores for living room and kitchen were around 60–70% during baseline. She was able to meet and surpass criterion levels in these rooms very quickly during intervention and maintained these gains during follow-up. Safety scores for mother's bedroom were well above 80% criterion level during baseline, while bathroom safety improved above 80% for the second observation, without targeted intervention.

Karen was involved in completing the revised Home Safety Checklist during observation and therefore was aware of the target changes in the bedroom and bathroom and behaviour generalised without further intervention. Both

bedroom and bathroom safety rose to and then remained at near 100% throughout the observation period.

After explanations of the dangers and hazards for her children, Karen was able to identify potential negative outcomes from existing hazards for her children and ensured that these were removed or fixed. For example, during baseline observations matches were found within the children's reach, Karen removed the matches to a safe area outside the children's reach and during any subsequent checks matches were never found within the children's reach again. In addition, Karen had not been aware of the potential risks of many choking hazards, for example, the fact that toys that were suitable for the older child could be classed as hazards for the younger child due to small parts. Once this was explained to Karen, she removed them out of the reach of the younger child.

Reductions in the level of home hazards were maintained at follow-up and Karen moved to a hostel with a lower level of staff support. The slight decrease in scores during the final two observations was due to the layout of the new accommodation, for example, there were no locked cupboards to store cleaning materials. Karen requested safety equipment to be provided by the hostel and consequently was able to make her new home safe for the children.

Cathleen's results show that although safety scores for living room and kitchen were around 60–70% during baseline, Cathleen was able to meet and surpass criterion levels in these rooms very quickly during intervention and maintained these gains during follow-up. Safety scores for the mother and children's bedrooms and bathroom were above 80% criterion level during baseline and improved without targeted intervention. Cathleen learned quickly to identify the potential hazardous outcomes for the children of being exposed to specific items.

One of the reasons for the relatively low frequency of hazards or dangers in the flat was the lack of material or personal possessions of Cathleen and the children. Cathleen's flat was sparsely furnished, containing very few items other than those provided by the project. Although Cathleen scored highly during safety checks, her children continued to suffer repeated minor bruises and injuries, for example, when unsupervised, her older son cut his foot by jumping off a bed onto a large toy. Cathleen's supervision of the children did not increase following these kinds of recurring injuries.

Cathleen decided to place both of her children into care and no follow-up data were available.

## Discussion

The Home Safety Programme Part 2 was effective with both mothers in reducing the levels of dangers in each targeted room of their flat, however, an increased awareness of dangers in the home did not generalise to improved supervision of children. This may have been due to both Karen and Cathleen's social isolation and diagnosis of depression. Both mothers had to balance the demands of two very young children who were close in age and both had recently separated from long-term relationships. Although their partners had been violent at times, they had offered a certain level of practical support in caring for the children.

Karen had intellectual disabilities and problems with literacy and numeracy. In addition, her older child was extremely active and required constant supervision. Both children presented as lively and happy. Children with behaviour problems have been found to be at increased risk of accidental injury, however in Karen's case it was the younger child who was at increased risk, because he was left unsupervised at times when Karen was focussing on the older child. Karen's children started to attend nursery midway through the intervention, allowing Karen time to complete household tasks without the children present. Intervention effects generalised across non-targeted rooms in the project flat as well as to Karen's new home in the community.

Supervision of both of Cathleen's children was patchy at times; for example, on several occasions Cathleen left both children alone in the flat while she was visiting other residents. Cathleen's children generally presented as bored and unhappy. About midway through the intervention, Cathleen's older child started attending nursery to ensure that he received adequate stimulation and allow Cathleen time to build her relationship with her younger child. However instead, Cathleen spent this time with other residents, largely ignoring her younger child.

## General discussion

The Home Safety Programme was implemented because there were considerable concerns about the children's safety in the project and some of the children had experienced repeated bruising and accidental injuries due to hazards within their reach or lack of supervision when being exposed to potentially dangerous situations. At the start of this programme all families lived in the project, in other words, in temporary accommodation. The flats were fully furnished and equipped and adhered to very strict health and safety guidelines that ensured that all equipment conformed to the highest safety standards. Any damaged or dangerous equipment was removed and replaced immediately by staff. Few of the parents in the project would be able to maintain these standards in their own homes. Furthermore, the families had been living in the project for a relatively short period of time and therefore had not accumulated many possessions of their own to fill their flat.

This programme effectively reduced the occurrences of home hazards for each of the families. Despite the fact that children at risk of neglect frequently experience minor accidental injury or bruising, the baseline measures of environmental hazards and dangers were already relatively low. This demonstrated that good standard accommodation can remove many risks and suggested that responsibility for child safety is not only the parent's but also requires responsible proprietors. Lynn, for example, made good progress while her family lived in the project but was unable to maintain this standard of home safety when she moved out into privately rented accommodation because she was not permitted by her landlord to make the necessary changes, for example, she was not allowed to put a safety latch on a cupboard door in the bathroom.

Parents were taught how to use safety equipment that was provided by the project, for example, socket guards and stair gates and subsequently used this equipment consistently. The provision of safety equipment was an important part of the programme; each flat had a lockable cupboard for the storage of hazardous items such as cleaning fluids. Young parents who live in the community are unlikely to have such safety items and may not have the finances to purchase or the skills to install safety equipment and require support in these basic areas of home safety.

This programme showed that even potentially intrusive observations such as staff checking cupboards and drawers were viewed by mothers as useful and supportive. All of the mothers willingly participated in the programme and none of them avoided any of the pre-arranged observation sessions. This was due at least in part to the fact that working in partnership with parents provided natural reinforcers, such as staff appreciation and praise for parents' involvement in completing the observation sheets and the provision of free safety equipment for the flat.

Cathleen's children experienced emotional neglect. Cathleen showed little interest in the children's welfare and did not engage with them even when supports were offered. This was in contrast to the other parents who may have lacked knowledge about their children's ability and development, but once they had this information provided good home safety. Cathleen's children's behaviour evidenced the impact of emotional neglect. They presented as unhappy, bored, and angry and showed little interest in their mother or other adults. Following their admission to foster care the children settled immediately and appeared happy and content. The elder child never asked for his mother.

While this programme focussed on home safety, the standard of hygiene in the home was not directly addressed. Since this was an issue for quite a few of the residents in the project, home hygiene was addressed and is described in the next chapter.

# CHAPTER 9

# Home Hygiene

Generally, hygiene standards vary widely across families and it is when these standards are harmful for the child, either physically or emotionally that this constitutes neglect. Very poor hygiene conditions in a home pose risks that can range from mild infections to serious health risks and are often an early indication of more general pervasive child care problems. For very young babies, serious health hazards such as fungal infections and diarrhoea can be the result of unhygienic preparation of baby milk formula. Later on, when babies tend to put everything in their reach into their mouth they can catch all sorts of infections through exposure to dirty kitchen floors, toilets, or other wet and unhygienic areas in a flat. This is particularly pertinent when babies become mobile, in other words, are able to crawl or toddle and come into direct contact with unclean surfaces or grubby toys or utensils.

Although older children may have developed a greater tolerance to bacteria and therefore experience fewer adverse health effects, the experience of poor personal or home hygiene is likely to affect them socially. Children who live in extremely dirty home environments and who have poor personal hygiene are likely to be rejected by their peers and the wider community, for example, they are less likely to be invited out or visited for play dates or are likely to be teased or bullied about being 'smelly'.

Child care workers generally are cautious about making value judgements about home hygiene because they do not want to be seen as discriminatory. However, there is a professional responsibility to decide at what point the condition of the home is likely to have an adverse effect on the child's wellbeing, in other words, at what point hygiene problems and poor housing are considered as part of serious neglect. Clearly there is a difference between inadequate living conditions caused by poverty and those caused by emotional neglect or lack of recognition of the children's basic needs. Furthermore, parental problems such as mental health, drug or alcohol abuse can lead to extreme cases of hygiene problems where child care workers have found human or animal faeces or rotting food lying around the home.

On the flipside, an environment that is kept obsessively sterile is not necessarily healthy, because it lacks the opportunity for the child's body to build up resistance to bacteria. The general increase in asthma and rhinitis is thought to be linked to children having less contact with microbes in the home and to eating more sterile foods.

In order to assess the quality of parenting it is necessary to find out if parents have the necessary knowledge and skills to meet their children's needs and whether or not they can consistently and routinely put these skills into practice. Occasional observations in the project showed that some mothers had extreme difficulty maintaining hygiene standards in the home and in some cases industrial cleaners had to be employed to clean the flats when the placement ended and families moved out from the project.

The Home Hygiene Programme was designed to develop an instrument to measure the standard of hygiene in the home, to assess if mothers have the skills to maintain standards of hygiene in their homes, to develop these skills if needed, through prompting, modelling and positive reinforcement, and to enable mothers to develop regular cleaning routines. This programme was conducted in 3 parts. Practice Tool 4 provides a workers' guide and the forms used for the Home Hygiene Programme.

## Part 1

### Susan

When Susan undertook work on the child care routines described earlier, it became evident that she had difficulty maintaining satisfactory hygiene standards in her home. The Home Hygiene Programme started two weeks later than work on routines. Home hygiene work finished because Susan's baby was taken into care under emergency child protection legislation.

Susan's baby was 5 weeks old at the start of this programme and had experienced diarrhoea that was possibly linked to poor hygiene. Susan had been able to maintain reasonable hygiene standards in her flat at the beginning of the placement, however as standards of overall child care decreased, so did standards of hygiene.

## Materials

The Checklist for Living Environments to Assess Neglect (CLEAN) (Watson-Perczel et al., 1988) was adapted for use in a residential project. The checklist measured the standard of the entire home in terms of three areas: cleanliness, inappropriately stored items, and clutter. Each room was graded according to levels of these three areas defined as follows:

1. *Clean or dirty*: the presence of organic matter on surfaces in each area of the flat;
2. *Clothing*: accumulations of clothing, towelling, bed clothes in each area of the flat;
3. *Clutter*: objects out of place in each area, for example, plates on the floor, socks on the kitchen table.

A task list was devised for each area and used as a visual prompt. Each item on the list was scored for *Clean* or *Dirty* on a scale from 10 for 'clean' to 0 for 'dirty'; for *Clothing* and *Clutter* on a scale from 5 for 'no items' to 0 for 'more than twenty items'. A percentage score for each category was calculated by taking the total score obtained divided by the total possible score multiplied by 100.

## Procedure

Observers were trained through verbal explanation of each of the items on the checklists and practice observations consisting of observers completing the check list independently in each room in a resident's flat. Interobserver agreement was above 91%. calculated using the following formula:

$$\frac{\text{Number of Agreements} \times 100}{\text{Number of Agreements} + \text{Number of Disagreements}}$$

The importance of a hygienic living environment for child health and development was explained to each participating mother. An initial baseline observation then was taken to assess existing standards of home hygiene. Following this initial baseline observation, the member of staff helped the mother to clean one room. This allowed the staff to see if the mother had the necessary

cleaning materials and skills to complete the task. If mothers did not have the necessary cleaning materials they were provided with them initially and the staff and the mother discussed and agreed which products she should purchase for future use. If the mother was unable to perform the task, the staff member offered verbal prompts followed by modelling, as necessary.

Following the initial session, weekly assessment observations were conducted at a pre-arranged time. A target room was selected for each week and the mother received the task list for the relevant room. During the assessment session, the mother accompanied the staff member and each item was discussed as it was scored. If the target room scored above 80% in all categories, an activity reinforcer was arranged with the mother, for example, going out for coffee with a staff member. If the target score was not reached, the member of staff and the mother undertook the cleaning of that area, using the checklist as a guideline. Intervention continued on each room until a target level of 80% was reached.

## Results

Although Susan scored above criterion levels in the categories Clutter and Clothing during baseline and throughout the intervention, she had difficulty maintaining levels of Cleanliness. While at first the living room was scored at 100% in the category Cleanliness, subsequent observations indicated that improvements were not maintained in this area. Soiled nappies and used baby wipes were often left on the floor or table tops and dirty ashtrays were spilt on the floor. There also was some initial improvement in the category Cleanliness in the kitchen where a score of 80% was recorded during the two subsequent observations. This was partly due to staff cleaning the kitchen between observations, as they were concerned about the potential impact on the baby's health. As Susan's placement ended no further observations were undertaken.

## Discussion

By the time intervention ended Susan was having difficulty in maintaining day-to-day routines for herself and the baby, as outlined in Chapter 7. Susan demonstrated during the very early weeks of the placement that she had the skills to maintain hygiene levels in her flat but was only able to sustain these for a short period. One difficulty was the amount of time Susan spent away from her flat, either out of the unit or with other residents, leaving her very little time to clean or tidy her flat or carry out child care tasks.

By-and-large, the assessment instrument was gauging the level of Cleanliness or hygiene throughout the flat, however the categories of Clutter and Clothing did not reflect standards in the flat entirely realistically. For example, when four soiled baby nappies were lying on the dining table, clearly posing a considerable health risk to both Susan and her baby, this resulted in a decrease of only 6% in the score on Clutter, leaving the score still well above the 80% criterion level. Informal field notes during this period often described the flat as very untidy, although this was not reflected in the results.

In addition, Susan's relatively positive scores in the categories Clutter and Clothing were more a reflection of the nature of the accommodation provided by the project than her ability to maintain acceptable home hygiene. Living in temporary accommodation meant that she only had a limited number of possessions and adequate storage spaces were provided.

The relative insensitivity of the assessment tool combined with field notes from the observers indicated that more specific information was necessary on what families needed to do to improve hygiene standards. In addition, the scoring scales also were too complex, making it difficult to fully involve some parents in completing the checklist. Therefore the checklist was modified in Parts 2 and Part 3.

## Part 2

## Ruby

Ruby had participated in previous work on feeding, bathing and routines. Ruby's child was 6 months old at the start of the Home Hygiene Programme and was beginning to spend more time on the floor, often with minimal supervision. The floors and furniture in Ruby's flat were often covered in old food and soiled nappies and dirty plates were frequently left on the floor. Ruby blamed her son for her flat being untidy or dirty, claiming that he did not like her to clean the flat and cried when she tried to do this. Although her son was becoming more mobile, for example, he

had begun to roll over when left on the floor, Ruby often refused to lift plates or cups off the floor, insisting that her son 'knew' not to touch them.

## Materials

The adjusted Checklist for Living Environments to Assess Neglect (CLEAN) that was used in Part 1 was revised further and individualised in Part 2. Scoring for specific items that could pose particular health risks, for example, floor surfaces, toilet, fridge, and bins, were added for each room and areas that needed to be cleaned or tidied at least once a week were identified. Other items were included that contributed to the overall standard in Ruby's flat.

The main emphasis of the checklist was shifted to Cleanliness, reducing the checkpoints relating to Clothing or Clutter and including them within the overall score rather than measuring them separately. In addition, a daily check list for each room was provided; this is included in Practice Tool 4.

## Procedure

The procedure used in Part 2 was the same as described in Part 1, with the exception that the updated checklist was used in the observations. Intervention continued in each room until the criterion level of 80% was reached for two observations. This is outlined in more detail in Practice Tool 4.

## Results

The intervention was initially successful in all rooms, however improvements were not maintained at follow-up. While a high rate of reinforcers were available Ruby had the skills to clean and tidy her flat, but this was not sustained when reinforcers were not readily available.

During the intervention phase in the living room Ruby scored 100% on two occasions, but this score decreased to a low of 50% during follow-up. Competing reinforcers available from other residents or friends inviting her to spend time away from the flat affected the home hygiene programme similar to the way this impacted on child care routines previously described.

The remaining problem areas were Ruby not washing dishes, keeping worktops clean, cleaning food spillages off the living room furniture, or tidying up dirty washing from the bedroom floor. The intervention ended when Ruby moved out of the project.

## Discussion

The revised instrument gave a more realistic overall picture of the condition of the home and therefore was useful in identifying specific areas that needed intervention. Vouchers, praise, and outings with staff acted as reinforcers for some areas but not others. The poor hygiene condition of Ruby's flat mirrored how she was coping with other child care tasks. On days when Ruby was focussed she met the targets however, on days when distracting and competing reinforcers were available in the form of friends asking her to go out, she became disorganised and the conditions in the flat deteriorated. The risks to the baby increased especially since he was becoming more mobile and spent considerable amounts of time on the floor unsupervised amongst dirty dishes and soiled nappies.

The multiple baseline record showed that intervention effects generalised from the targeted room to all rooms, for example during intervention for the kitchen, home hygiene also improved in the bathroom and living room to 100%. However, generalisation effects were also observed when the intervention was not effective, for example, the seventh observation showed low scores for both the kitchen and bathroom. In general, standards were similar in all rooms regardless of the intervention phase.

Because results generalised throughout the flat, targeting each room in sequence may not have been necessary. This is explored in Part 3.

## Part 3

## Cathleen

Cathleen had taken part in the Home Safety Programme. Her children were 1 and 3 years of age. She was included in the programme because she had difficulty in maintaining hygiene standards in her flat. Cathleen often left the children unattended while they were eating and as a result the younger child frequently spilled food on the floor and over his highchair, which was often left for several days and got mouldy, before being cleaned.

Cathleen had lived independently in the community prior to the children being admitted to care. There were serious concerns about the standard of hygiene in her home, for example, staff reported that rotting food and used nappies were strewn on the floor. An indication of the unhygienic state of her flat was that when Cathleen left her community home many items including furniture and carpets had to be burned because they were in such an unhygienic condition.

## Karen

Karen had taken part in the Home Safety Programme; her children were 1 and 2 years old. Although Karen cleaned her flat on a regular basis, the flat often presented as untidy and dirty with spilled food. Karen had attempted to toilet train her older son for several weeks and he had had several 'accidents' on the carpet in the flat. Unhygienic conditions were particularly dangerous for Karen's younger son who had asthma and regularly had to use an inhaler.

## Hannah

Hannah was 17 years of age when she was admitted to the project prior to the birth of her baby. Hannah had spent most of her life in care, most recently in a children's home. Although she had some contact with her parents this was sporadic and not always supportive. Hannah was referred to the project because she was very young and inexperienced in looking after children. Hannah's child care skills and routines were assessed using the methods and practice tools as outlined in Chapters 6 and 7. She required no help in these areas.

In relation to standards of tidiness and hygiene within the home, initially Hannah maintained high standards however they dropped significantly following the birth of the baby. Therefore she was included in the Home Hygiene Programme.

## Materials

The checklist was the same as that described in Part 2.

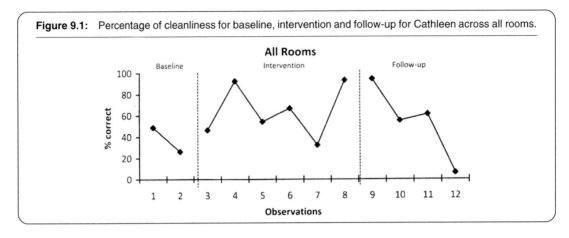

**Figure 9.1:**   Percentage of cleanliness for baseline, intervention and follow-up for Cathleen across all rooms.

## Procedure

The procedure was the same as that outlined in Part 1 apart from the following adaptations; the entire flat was used as a target area, rather than individual rooms as in Part 1. However, room specific data collection was continued. Two baseline observations were undertaken. Staff helped the mothers to clean one room following the second baseline observation (modelling). Vouchers were used as in Part 1, and follow-up data were collected weekly throughout the duration of the placement.

An AB and follow-up design was implemented for two mothers. Follow up data were not available for Karen, because hygiene standards did not reach criterion levels on two consecutive observations in all rooms during the placement.

## Results – Cathleen

During baseline observations Cathleen had no cleaning products in her flat and did not know what to buy. Figure 9.1 shows that scores were above baseline levels on two occasions during intervention and once during follow-up, but these scores were not sustained consistently. Each of these high scores coincided with Case Conferences, when Cathleen was aware that professionals would be making decisions about whether or not the placement of her children with her should continue because of child care concerns.

As in Parts 1 and 2 of this programme, data followed a similar pattern with high scores in one area generalised to other areas. Low scores were repeated across rooms.

The area that Cathleen made most progress in was the living room, reaching 100% during two observations. The children's comfort was not always a concern for Cathleen, for example Cathleen rarely had clean towels for the children, which meant that after baths they were often dried with damp towels. The children's bedding was often soiled and unchanged. As Cathleen's children were both mobile, they were under increased risk of infection through touching items which were dirty, for example the toilet, particularly as the children were at times unsupervised. The toilet continued to be unclean during 33% of observations during intervention. Cathleen reported that she found it difficult to clean the flat and supervise her children; however when a nursery placement was provided for her eldest child standards in the home did not improve. During follow-up standards in the flat deteriorated; this coincided with Cathleen's decision to place the children in foster care.

## Results – Karen

Although home hygiene scores for Karen increased following baseline the intervention continued because criterion levels were reached only on one occasion in all rooms. Although progress was maintained in the bedrooms, low scores for cleanliness in the kitchen due to dirty dishes and bins posed a particular risk of infection since the children were unsupervised at times and were mobile enough to access bins and the sink.

Karen found it difficult to clean her flat while at the same time supervising the children, and home hygiene improved somewhat when the older boy began to attend nursery school. However, scores were very low in the fourth observation. This observation coincided with Karen's son being off nursery on his mid-term break and highlighted the difficulty Karen had in maintaining hygiene standards while supervising both children. Eventually, scores improved when Karen completed the cleaning tasks at times when her younger son had a nap. Low scores during the final observation reflected the fact that Karen was packing up the flat to move to new accommodation.

## Results – Hannah

Hannah's scores for home hygiene surpassed criterion levels during intervention, but were not maintained at follow-up. Hannah's scores for individual rooms showed that she had most difficulty maintaining home hygiene in the kitchen. Dirty dishes and worktops in the kitchen posed a health risk, especially since Hannah prepared baby bottles in this less than hygienic environment. The area where most progress was made was the living room. Although scores for this area dropped during follow-up these were still at the 80% criterion level.

## Discussion

When all rooms in the flat were targeted simultaneously for home hygiene interventions, all three mothers reached criterion levels for all rooms on at least one occasion, however levels of home hygiene were not maintained across time. Cathleen and Karen needed to clean their flats more frequently than Hannah because they each had two children who were older and more mobile. Their children were exposed to a higher risk of infection than Hannah's baby because they were able to gain direct contact to areas that were unclean throughout the flats.

At the same time, older children actively contributed to untidiness in the flat, for example, by not tidying up toys after playing or by leaving food remains around the flat. Although home hygiene scores for Karen did not always reach criterion levels, the increase in scores reflected her attempts to maintain hygiene in her flat that could have reached criterion levels if intervention had continued, however this was not possible after Karen moved out of the project.

## General discussion

Although staff had reported low levels of home hygiene, this was not fully reflected in the scores obtained with the CLEAN checklist. The CLEAN checklist effectively measured the levels of Cleanliness, yet measures of Clutter and Clothing were not relevant for participating families who lived in temporary accommodation because they had fewer possessions than families who live in long-term homes. In addition, the families with very young babies had fewer toys and books than the families with older children.

The revised checklist gave a more realistic picture of the reality in the flats and included explicit home hygiene targets. The revised checklist differed from other existing measures of home conditions because it was based entirely on positive non-judgemental statements making it highly acceptable to parents and designed to be completed by and/or with parents, ensuring participation and empowerment. Both of these improvements meant that even mandated home hygiene checks were acceptable for these families.

All participants reached criterion levels at some point during the intervention phase. This means that standards were realistic and skills deficits were appropriately addressed through modelling and verbal instruction. However, planned reinforcers such as social outings or other activities with staff, had a limited effect. Modelling, including staff showing mothers how to clean their flat, inadvertently functioned to reinforce 'not cleaning the flat' until staff were present and thus maintenance of progress became problematic.

Clearly, mothers who provide adequate care for her child, like Hannah who was the only parent whose child was not on the child protection register, did better in the home hygiene programme while mothers who had more general difficulty with caring for their children also had problems with home hygiene. These findings may indicate that something that can be assessed quite easily such as standards of home hygiene can be used to assess overall standards of child care. Low levels of home hygiene can be used as an indicator of general child neglect because in this case omission of care behaviours leaves a measurable product of behaviour.

Of course, home hygiene needs to be considered in the context of the age and developmental level of the child. For example, Ruby did not realise that a baby who could roll would be able to reach unhygienic items that were lying on the floor. Furthermore, risks may not always be obvious, such as a work surface in the kitchen that may appear to be clean but if it has been wiped with a dirty cloth, poses a high hygiene risks.

Poor hygiene in the home is often attributed to poverty and low standards of housing; however this programme showed that even where accommodation is of a high standard other factors can influence the condition of the flat, such as time spent away from the flat or difficulties of completing household tasks while supervising the children. A parent's intellectual capacity was less of an issue, as seen in Karen who was diagnosed with intellectual disability that may have slowed down her progress, however, she was able to learn and maintain home hygiene routines.

Finally, unhygienic home conditions may be considered neglect even if they are not very severe, for example, Hannah's flat generally could have been considered adequate, but was a source of infection for the baby because of unhygienic conditions in the kitchen.

# CHAPTER 10

# Parent–Child Interaction

Chapters 6 and 7 highlighted the difficulties parents had in recognising and responding sensitively to infant cues; it became apparent that child responses did not have much of an effect on parent behaviours. Some parents had problems in ensuring safety and hygiene standards for their children in the home, despite being aware of the direct impact that this could have on their child's health, for example that a baby's diarrhoea was caused by unhygienic living conditions.

Clearly for many of these vulnerable mothers, the child's wellbeing did not function as a positive reinforcer for adequate parental caretaking behaviour. Furthermore, the child's distress or discomfort did not function to decrease behaviours incompatible with taking care of the child. In order to establish infant responses as reinforcers for parenting behaviours, this programme focussed on teaching parents to 'read' and respond contingently to their child's cues.

Very young parents, especially if they grew up in care and therefore had limited experience of appropriate parenting during their own childhood or experienced additional external stress, can find interactions with their child difficult to manage. Many of the mothers in the project were unable to 'read' the child's cues, such that they were not able to distinguish between a baby's cries because it was hungry, hurt, or tired, or they simply did not know enough about child development to have the appropriate expectations of what the baby can or cannot do and how to provide adequate stimulation.

On the other hand, responses from the child to parental caregiving were misinterpreted, for example, some of the mothers stated that they felt their baby 'rejected' or 'disliked' them when the baby cried, rather than considering baby cries as expressions of baby needs. At the same time, the baby's 'happy' sounds were not interpreted as a consequence of having met all their baby's needs and thus did not function as reinforcers for appropriate child care behaviour.

The issues addressed in this chapter related to the interaction between parents and their child, with a particular focus on teaching parents to 'read' their baby's cues and respond

appropriately. Parent education methods devised by Feldman (1994) were adapted and developed to improve interaction between parents and children in a way that was easily understood by parents of all levels of ability. The programme is reported in two parts to reflect the development of the instruments. More detailed workers' guidance and materials can be found in Practice Tool 5.

## Part 1

### Evelyn

Evelyn had intellectual disabilities and attended the project for two full days per week while waiting for a residential place to become available for her. Evelyn spent the rest of the week in the community, with daily support from professionals and extended family.

Initial assessment outlined in the first programme in Chapter 7 showed that Evelyn was able to perform basic child care tasks, including cleaning and preparing bottles, feeding, and changing a nappy at the target level of 80% correct and therefore required no intervention in these areas. Evelyn received advice and training in other child care skills that were not targeted for specific intervention, included weaning, nutrition, and cooking.

Evelyn received behavioural parent education related to child care skills for bathing her baby and while these skills improved quite quickly and remained at 100% during follow-up, this was achieved using extraneous arbitrary reinforcers. The baby's wellbeing did not function as a natural reinforcer for Evelyn's child care behaviours.

Furthermore, Evelyn's child care skills assessment indicated that 'talking to and maintaining eye contact with the baby' happened at very low rates. Evelyn rarely talked to or looked at her baby unless the baby was crying. Attending to more than one task at any a time was difficult for Evelyn and she generally completed each task before starting the next, for example, if the baby began crying while a member of staff was talking to Evelyn, she waited until the member of staff had stopped talking before responding to the baby. This became a problem especially in the early weeks after she moved into the project when the baby was very unsettled and cried frequently. Evelyn was included in Part 1 to enhance her interaction with her baby.

## Measures

Definitions of target behaviour were based on Feldman's (1994) definitions of key interaction behaviours:

1. *Mother imitates child vocalisation* – mother repeats, approximates or expands any noises that the child makes, within 5 seconds.
2. *Mother praises child* – any positive comment directed to the child that expresses approval contingent on something the child does.
3. *Mother gives physical affection* – any hugs, kisses, strokes, or tickles.
4. *Mother prompts child to play* – mother provides verbal or physical prompts to encourage her child to play, or any interactional play.
5. *Mother talks to child* – verbalisations directed at child, in a gentle or playful tone, including rhymes or songs. This does not include any critical comments.
6. *Mother looks at child* – mother faces the child for at least two seconds. (p. 391–2)

Feldman et al. (1986) provided target mean scores for appropriate parent-child interaction of 30% for the first three target responses, imitation, praise, and physical affection, and 80% for the next three targets, prompting, talking, and looking at the baby. These benchmarks for parents without intellectual disabilities reflected the natural variations in rates of maternal behaviour during interaction and therefore were adopted as target scores for this programme.

The baby's behaviour was not directly targeted during intervention, but was used to provide feedback to mothers about their responsiveness to the baby. Two of Feldman et al.'s (1993: 391–2) baby interaction behaviours were included:

1. *Child vocalises* – any vocal sound coming from the child except crying, burping or screaming.
2. *Child plays* – child uses toy for intended purpose or any interactional play.

A third category was included based on the data collected in the programmes so far in which many of the mothers did not look at the baby while they were involved in child care tasks, and therefore did not see whether or not the baby looked at them:

3. *Child looks at parent* – Child looks at mother for at least 2 seconds.

## Procedure

Observations took place within the communal living room in the project. Observations were recorded on video and scored using a partial-interval recording schedule of 20-second intervals. Each of the target behaviours was recorded with a tick (✓) if it occurred during the 20-second interval without prompting from the observer.

A multiple baseline across behaviours design was used; each behaviour was targeted once criterion levels for the previously targeted behaviour had been reached.

Observers were trained using a video recording of interactions between a mother and her child, who were not included in this programme. Observations were recorded on a sheet based on the Step-by-Step Child Care Manual (Feldman & Case, 1993) (see Practice Tool 5).

Inter-observer agreement was calculated on 48% of observations by two observers across all behaviours. Mean overall agreement was 87%, and ranged from 75–95%.

Staff explained the intervention process to Evelyn as a way of helping mothers and babies to communicate better with each other. The residential child care worker who had conducted the earlier observations of Evelyn's child care tasks and who was familiar with Evelyn and her baby was trained in the procedure and recorded all observations on video.

Observations were scheduled for 5 minutes twice a week over period of 3 months, starting when the baby was 10 weeks old. Observation sessions were scheduled when the baby was alert and settled; if the baby became unsettled during an observation, the observation was postponed.

During baseline observations Evelyn was asked to play with the baby in the way that she normally would. No prompting, modelling, or feedback was provided during the baseline phase other than thanking Evelyn for participating. The observer did not interact with Evelyn or the baby during observations. After a stable baseline was established, behaviours that did not reach criterion levels were targeted for intervention, one at a time.

Intervention involved modelling, rehearsal, discussion, and feedback on the performance of the target behaviour. The staff member explained to Evelyn why each particular target behaviour was important, and then modelled the behaviour. She then asked Evelyn to demonstrate the behaviour and praised her for a correct response. Evelyn was advised on the use of developmentally appropriate toys and rhymes. Evelyn received a homework chart to act as a prompt to remind her to practice the behaviour between sessions at home. She was prompted regularly to practice specific target behaviours during the intervention phase and praised for correct performances. When the behaviour reached criterion levels over three observations, the intervention was discontinued for that particular behaviour and a new target behaviour was selected for intervention.

During the follow-up period, if a behaviour was recorded at zero level, booster sessions were implemented, using the same intervention strategies. The baby's response rate was used as feedback for Evelyn, by drawing Evelyn's attention to and praising her for increases in the baby's vocalisation, eye contact, and play behaviour immediately following sessions and prior to commencing the next observation.

## Results

Figure 10.1 shows results for all targeted behaviours. *Imitation* increased from 0% during baseline to a mean criterion of 33% during the intervention phase. This was not maintained during the follow-up phase when the mean score fell to 12.5%. As the behaviour fell to 0% on two observation sessions a booster session was implemented, after which a mean score of 31% was maintained which was just above the target level of 30%. During later observations when the baby's vocalisations became more complex, Evelyn continued to imitate using sounds that resembled those that the baby had been making during the early observations.

*Praise* was the second target behaviour and increased from 0% during baseline to a mean rate of 46% during intervention. During the initial follow-up period the mean score was 29%. The score was 0% during the sixteenth observation, therefore a booster session was provided. During the second follow-up phase a mean score of 34% was maintained. However, at times praise was not

contingent on the baby's behaviour, in other words, Evelyn praised her baby non-specifically such as simply saying 'great girl' with no specific child behaviour setting the occasion for this response. At other times praise was contingent on the baby's behaviour but appeared excessive. Additional advice was provided on appropriate and timely delivery of praise.

The target behaviour *mother shows physical affection* exceeded the mean criterion of 30% during baseline and therefore was not targeted for intervention.

The next behaviour to be targeted was *prompting play*. Evelyn was encouraged to use the baby's own toys and staff modelled age appropriate play with the baby. Evelyn knew a range of interactive baby rhymes and was able to use these appropriately. Although Evelyn's performance in this skill improved from a baseline mean of 8% to 30% during intervention, Evelyn was unable to reach the criterion level of 80%. Consequently, intervention for play behaviour continued until Evelyn's placement ended. The target behaviours *mother talks to child*, and *mother looks at child* required no intervention; both behaviours surpassed the 80% criterion level during baseline observations.

With regard to child behaviours, the baby did not vocalise during baseline but rates of *baby vocalisation* increased in direct correspondence with increases in mother's imitation of baby vocalisations. The rates of the *baby looking at mother* increased after the first two observations. During the tenth observation when Evelyn did not imitate vocalisations, the baby did not look at Evelyn. During later observations the baby was becoming more active and able to roll and at times did not look at Evelyn because she was distracted by the camera and the observer.

Although Evelyn stated that she was completing her homework charts she did not return them to the main observer, so it seems unlikely that these were completed.

## Discussion

It was evident during intervention that external environmental factors impacted on Evelyn's interaction with the baby, for example, when she had difficulties with her extended family during the tenth observation day, she did not imitate or show physical affection for the baby. The child vocalised less and did not look at Evelyn

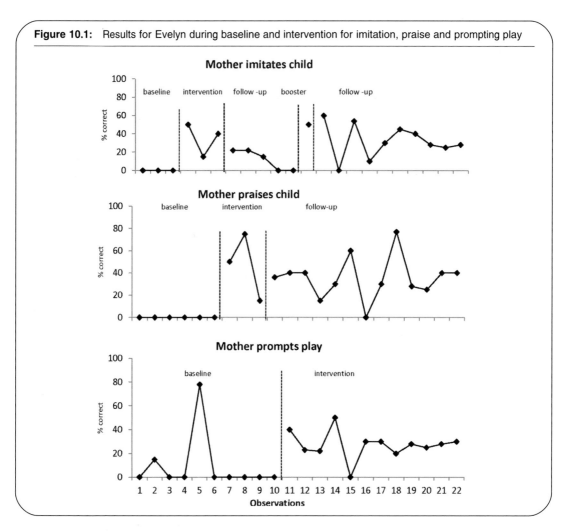

**Figure 10.1:**    Results for Evelyn during baseline and intervention for imitation, praise and prompting play

throughout that observation period. However, increasingly when Evelyn did not perform a target behaviour she was able to identify the things she had 'forgotten to do' and engaged in the 'missed' behaviour immediately after the observation.

It is possible that the presence of an observer acted as a discriminative stimulus for performing behaviours and that the targeted behaviours did not generalise to other times of the day. Although Evelyn had agreed to self-record she did not do so and it is unclear whether or not she engaged in target behaviours between observation and training sessions. Given the fluctuating rates of performance of each skill and the need for booster sessions, it seems likely that she did not engage in target behaviours outside of observation sessions.

Although Part 1 showed an increase in target behaviours and child responses it did not address the quality or sensitivity of the mother's

responses; for example, during some observations Evelyn responded very sensitively to the baby, talking to her in a quiet way, with gentle movements when the baby was tired and ready for a nap. During observations when Evelyn was responding appropriately to the baby, she described the baby's behaviour, making comments like 'oh you're tired', or asking questions like 'do you want to play with that?' when the baby looked at a toy. On other occasions Evelyn's interaction were inappropriately intrusive; she was trying to stimulate the baby and encouraging her to play when the baby was clearly tired and was averting her gaze from her mother. Although this was discussed with Evelyn at the time, it was not reflected in the data collected in Part 1 and therefore this was addressed in Part 2 of the parent child interaction programme.

## Part 2

## Mary

Mary was 18 years old when she was referred to the project 4 weeks prior to the birth of her son. She had spent most of her life in care following physical and sexual abuse by her parents. Mary had not had any contact with her parents for a number of years, however contact resumed when she was pregnant and subsequently Mary experienced further physical abuse by her mother. The baby's father had sexually abused young children and therefore was not allowed any contact with the baby. Mary's baby was placed on the child protection register at birth under the category of potential neglect.

Mary was referred to the project because of concerns about her nomadic lifestyle and difficulty in looking after herself. Mary had had difficulty settling in previous accommodation, often not unpacking her possessions and living out of carrier bags. Professionals were concerned about Mary's vulnerability within relationships and the risks posed by Mary's family. Mary had a support network of friends and professionals who she saw regularly.

Although Mary was initially reluctant to move into the project, after the first two weeks she appeared to settle well and began to form relationships with project staff. Throughout her placement Mary stated that she wished to live independently in the community with her child, however Mary's behaviour indicated that she was extremely anxious about the move. This behaviour included avoiding any work addressing the move into the community and at one stage accepting accommodation that was unsuitable in the knowledge that professionals would advise her not to move.

Mary's baby was 3 months old at the beginning of the work on parent child interaction. Mary's basic child care skills had been assessed and had reached criterion levels for all skills. Mary had well-established routines for her son and therefore did not take part in any of the previously described programmes.

Informal observations by project staff highlighted that Mary was at times insensitive in her interaction with the baby, for example, throwing him in the air in a way that appeared to frighten the baby and then laughing at his reaction. Generally, Mary appeared to be unable to read the baby's responses especially when he seemed frightened or distressed. At times Mary said that she felt uncomfortable talking to the baby and the baby was not vocalising. Mary had difficulty comforting the baby when he was unsettled and often asked staff to comfort him, saying that she could not cope and was frightened that she might hurt him if he did not stop crying.

Mary was due to move into her own accommodation during the period when observations took place and agreed that observations could continue in her new home. Mary was enthusiastic about completing observations, often asking when the next one would be done. She was keen that other members of staff who were not involved in observations watched her videos.

## Alice

Alice was 18 years old when she moved to the project with her new born baby. Alice experienced neglect, and physical and sexual abuse during own childhood. She left home aged 13 years of age and lived with various members of her extended family. Although Social Services investigated the sexual abuse allegations, no action was taken and Alice felt that no one believed her. She got involved in solvent and alcohol misuse, began to self-harm, and on a number of occasions, took an overdose of sleeping tablets. She was hospitalised for depression and did not comply with her medication regime.

Alice experienced severe domestic violence within her adult relationships with men. Her last two partners had assaulted her so severely that she was admitted to hospital. She was referred to the project because of concerns about her ability to protect herself and her son. Alice intended to continue her relationship with her partner in spite of the violence and denied that he posed a risk to her child.

Alice experienced extreme and unpredictable mood swings: at times she presented as extremely angry while at other times she was elated. Staff were concerned that Alice's baby would be at risk during her angry moods, but Alice did not share these concerns.

Alice met her baby's physical needs and performed all child care tasks to a high standard. Alice's baby presented as withdrawn and difficult to engage. Although the baby was 3 months old at the start of interaction work, he rarely vocalised and often was irritable. Alice took part to assess the quality of her interaction with the baby and to give her the opportunity to see how her behaviour impacted on baby's responses.

Alice's baby was on the Child Protection Register under the categories of neglect and potential physical abuse and was also subject to an Interim Care Order.

## Materials

Target behaviour the Parent–Child Interaction Programme Part 2 included all target behaviours used in Part 1. Two categories of behaviour were added and defined as follows:

- *Child positive expression* – Child smiles, in other words, child's mouth turns up at the corners, mouth is either open or closed.
- *Mother reads the baby* – mother appropriately describes baby's state, for example 'you're tired, hungry, bored' etc. or mother gives the baby an appropriate dialogue for example 'you're telling me that you want to play'.

*Child positive expression* was added to reflect the baby's overall mood, give feedback to mothers on their child's enjoyment of interaction, and strengthen positive reinforcer value provided by the baby's responses, such as smiles or laughs, to appropriate parental behaviour. Given the difficulties that Evelyn had in Part 1 in identifying and reacting to the baby's moods and conditions appropriately, the category *mother reads baby* was added to improve the parent's ability to 'read' the baby's overall mood, strengthen their sensitivity to cues from the baby, and subsequently ensure appropriate parental response.

Since there were no existing benchmark scores for these two new behavioural categories as they did not exist in Feldman's scoring system, criterion levels were set at 30%, the same as other lower-rate behaviours praise, imitation, and physical affection. Using an abridged version of Ainsworth's Sensitivity Scale (Ainsworth, Bell & Stayton, 1974), sensitivity was scored between 1–9 for all behaviour categories during observations as follows:

- *9 Highly sensitive*
  Mother responds promptly and appropriately to her baby's signals.
- *7 Sensitive*
  Mother responds promptly and appropriately to her baby's signals, but sometimes becomes distracted and misses the baby's cues.

- *5 Inconsistently sensitive*
  Mother is prompt and responsive to infant cues on some occasions, but either inappropriate or slow at other times.
- *3 Insensitive*
  Mother is inaccessible or misinterprets the baby's signals. Responses are often delayed or inappropriate, but if the baby's mood and activity match the mother's she shows some sensitivity.
- *1 Highly Insensitive*
  Mother is geared almost exclusively to her own wishes. Her response to the infants signal is delayed and inappropriate.

Sensitivity was defined as 'the mother's ability to perceive and to interpret accurately the signals and communications implicit in her infant's behaviour, and given this understanding, to respond to them appropriately and promptly' (Ainsworth et al., 1974: 127). In other words, the mother noticed the child's signal and responded appropriately and promptly.

Interobserver agreement was calculated using the same formula used in the first part of the programme. Interobserver agreement for Mary's behaviour was calculated for 70% of observations by two observers across all behaviours. Mean overall agreement was 94%, and ranged from 92–97%.

Interobserver agreement was calculated on 80% of observations for Alice. Mean agreement was 94.5% and ranged from 93%–97%. Interobserver agreement on the sensitivity scale was 100% for both mothers.

## Procedure

Part 2 following the same procedure as Parent–Child Interaction Programme Part 1, without the requirement to complete homework charts, as these were ineffective during the first part of the programme.

Part 2 of the programme included the additional behavioural categories described above. A multiple baseline across behaviours design was used and each observation session was given an overall rating regarding sensitivity. Baseline measures for maternal behaviours were taken on *praise, prompting play, talking to the baby, looking at the baby, imitation, showing physical affection* and *reading the baby*. Baseline measures for infant behaviour were taken on *vocalising, playing, looking at parent* and *positive expression*.

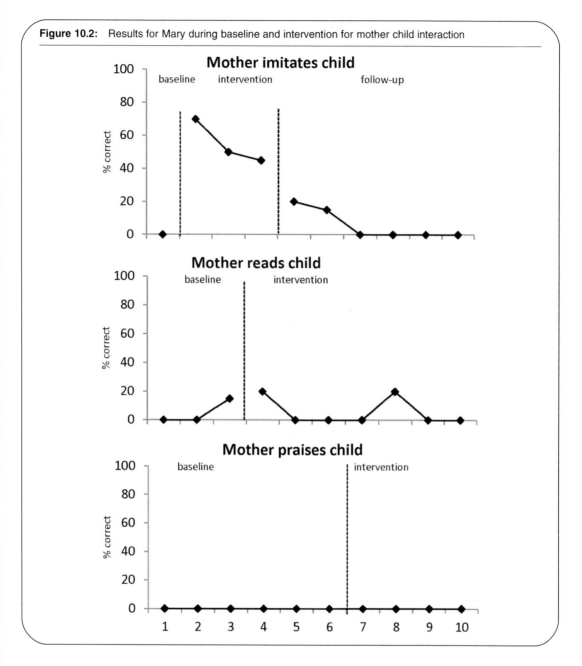

**Figure 10.2:** Results for Mary during baseline and intervention for mother child interaction

The intervention methods outlined in Part 1 of this programme were used including modelling, rehearsal, discussion, and feedback regarding the video recording. This meant that a staff member reviewed the videos with the mother and encouraged her to observe the target behaviour and the baby's responses.

Intervention to address *reading the baby* took the form of asking the mothers to give the baby a 'dialogue' while watching videos. Mothers were asked, 'If your baby could speak what would he say?' If mothers were unable to do this, the observer modelled the behaviour.

### Results

Figure 10.2 shows the results for Mary during baseline, intervention, and follow up for *imitation*, and during baseline and intervention for *reading* the baby and *praising the baby*. Imitation increased from 0% during baseline to a mean of 59% during intervention. The other behaviours remain at baseline levels. As the baby was vocalising during baseline observations there were opportunities for imitation, however, maternal imitation was not maintained at follow-up when rates fell back to 0% and so a booster session was implemented. During the final two follow-up sessions the rates remained at 0%.

*Reading the baby* was the second behaviour to be targeted. During intervention Mary did not give the baby an appropriate dialogue and although a member of staff modelled this, Mary was unable to imitate and consistently put her baby's condition into words. Reading the baby was scored at 20% on two occasions.

*Praise* was the third behaviour to be targeted and although this was rehearsed repeatedly and the importance of this behaviour was pointed out to Mary, she did not perform this behaviour during observations.

*Sensitivity* ratings ranged from 1 to 5, the mean score was 3. Behaviours resulting in a low sensitivity score included failing to comfort the baby when he was unhappy, continuing to playfully bite the baby's feet or tickle the baby when he was unhappy and not responding to this interaction, pulling the baby's hands out of his mouth when he was teething and wanted to chew them, ignoring the baby's attempt to hold toys, and instead presenting him with alternative toys chosen by Mary.

Mary identified some of her inappropriate responses to the baby when reviewing the videos. These tended to be the most obvious responses, which resulted in the baby crying, rather than the more subtle incidents when the baby showed discomfort. In spite of being able to identify inappropriate responses, Mary's interaction with her baby did not change.

*Looking at the baby*, *prompting play* and *talking to the baby* all reached criterion levels at baseline and required no intervention. *Showing physical affection* towards the baby had a mean score of 36% and appeared to be linked to the baby's positive expression and therefore did not require separate intervention.

*Child vocalisation* showed an initial increase in line with increases in *mother's imitation*; however, it decreased as the rate of maternal imitation decreased. The reduction in the rate of *child looks at parent* were partly caused by Mary prompting the baby to play during observations therefore the

baby's attention was focused on the toy rather than the mother. There also was a noticeable downward trend in scores for *child's positive expression* due to the lack of contingent maternal attention.

After ten observations Mary and her baby moved into the community and it was not possible to continue with observations as planned. Two days after their move, the baby was taken into care on a voluntary basis, following the disclosure that Mary had allowed the baby to have contact with a person who was known to have sexually abused children.

## Discussion

Overall, there was very little increase in the target behaviours for Mary and her baby. Although *talking to the baby* and *prompting play* occurred at appropriate frequencies and thus required no intervention, there was a lack of sensitivity in relation to both behaviours; for example, Mary frequently ignored cues from the baby in relation to play and removed him from toys he was interested in and expected him to play with toys that she had selected.

While the intervention was not successful in increasing and maintaining target behaviour, it provided useful assessment data on the quality of interaction between Mary and her baby, in particular the difficulties with sensitivity. Encouraging Mary to put in words how the baby was feeling by giving the baby a dialogue allowed her to recognise some of her non-contingent responses to the baby and to notice the child's positive responses.

The results reflected concerns expressed by the staff team about the baby's general presentation during this period; the baby gradually became more and more withdrawn and frequently appeared to be unhappy. Previously satisfactory standards of day-to-day child care deteriorated and while Mary was willing to participate in the videos, the feedback she received did not function to improve sensitivity of child related behaviours.

## Alice

As Alice participated in only 5 observation sessions before withdrawing from intervention; no follow-up data were available. *Praise* was the first target behaviour. Alice reached criterion scores following two observations and was able to give examples of the importance of praise in managing children's behaviour, stating that she had observed her sister using praise with Alice's 3 year old nephew.

Although *imitation* occurred at low rates during the first two baseline observations, scores dropped to 0% prior to intervention. In reviewing the video, Alice was able to identify the decrease in her son's vocalisation when her rate of imitation decreased and subsequently scored a mean of 47% during the intervention phase for imitation. Increases in the child's responsive behaviour reflected the increases in maternal imitation.

During baseline *looking at the baby* was observed at 100% and *physical affection* had a mean score of 32%, *talking to the baby* was scored at 95%, and *reading the baby* scored 32%. As each of these target behaviours were observed at percentages well above the target score, no further intervention was required. Staff delivered verbal praise for Alice's performances on these behaviours.

With regard to *sensitivity* the maximum score of 9 was recorded throughout all observations. Alice was very responsive to her baby and reacted immediately to signs of boredom or frustration by distracting the baby, for example, presenting a toy to the baby. *Reading the baby* was also observed at a high rate, for example, Alice frequently made appropriate comments that showed an understanding of the baby's state such as 'you're fed-up' or asking 'do you want to play with that?' when the baby looked at a toy.

## Discussion

Although Alice's results showed positive interaction with the baby, she frequently cancelled pre-arranged observation sessions, especially when she was feeling angry or depressed which usually happened following an argument with her partner. Informal observations indicated that Alice interacted very little with the baby when she was preoccupied with these kinds of external events.

The increases in target behaviours that were maintained between sessions suggested that Alice was able to retain the skills she had learned in the intervention. Alice clearly enjoyed the Programme and often asked other members of staff to watch her videos. Yet, Alice withdrew after only 5 observation sessions due to difficulties in her relationships with her family and her partner.

## General discussion

A number of common themes emerged from the Parent–Child Interaction Programme. While this programme initially used a procedure specifically developed for parents with intellectual disabilities, the findings of Part 1 match Feldman et al.'s (1986) findings that some parents with intellectual disabilities tend to praise and imitate their babies at low rates. However, Part 2 of this programme showed that participating mothers who did not have intellectual disabilities also showed low baseline rates of these behaviours. Consequently, it seems that the factors that prevent mothers from learning these pivotal child care responses are not related to their own intellectual ability.

In this programme, all three mothers had difficult childhood experiences, suffered maltreatment, neglect, and/or abuse perpetrated by one or both of their parents, and continued to have difficulties in their relationships with their parents. It seemed likely that each mother's lack of opportunity to observe or experience consistent positive parenting while growing up may have contributed to later difficulties in interaction with their own children.

Evelyn and Mary both had few opportunities to care for younger siblings or other young children. Evelyn had very limited opportunities to look after any children as her mother did not believe that Evelyn was capable of looking after herself much less caring for a child. Mary spent most of her life in care, largely in children's homes, where she would have had limited contact with young children or their carers. In contrast Alice had an older sister with a young child, who would have given her opportunities for observational learning; this was reflected in Alice's baseline scores for all behaviours, which were higher than those of the other two mothers.

This programme demonstrates that interaction skills can be learned if parents do not have the skills in their repertoires, but also how stress can impact on parent-child interaction. For example, Mary's fears about moving into the community resulted in her becoming increasingly withdrawn from her child; Evelyn's scores dropped for all behaviours on a day when she had difficulties in relationships with her wider family. When Evelyn's difficulties were resolved in time for the following observation scores increased. Alice withdrew from the procedure completely when she was having difficulties with her family, so it was not possible to explore the effect of this on her interaction.

Part 1 of the programme showed increases in targeted maternal behaviour and the subsequent impact on child behaviour, but did not address the overall sensitivity of the interaction. The addition of the sensitivity scale in Part 2 of the programme addressed this and although it gave an overall score rather than a separate score for each specific target behaviours, the high level of interobserver agreement indicated that this was a useful tool for assessing sensitivity.

A link emerged between overall sensitivity and the mother's ability to *read the baby*, for example, Alice was sensitive to her child during all observations and also scored well on *reading the baby* without intervention. Mary in contrast obtained low scores on sensitivity and was only able to *read the baby* during two observations, despite the intervention.

The addition of the *child's positive expression* was a useful tool for providing feedback to Alice and strengthened the reinforcement value of the child's reaction, as Alice was praised by staff when her child smiled. This did not appear to have been effective with Mary; her child's behaviour did not function strongly as reinforcer for her child care behaviours, even after intervention.

The impact of the mother's behaviour on the child's development in relation to vocalisation was evident with all participants; the rate of vocalisation of both Evelyn's and Alice's babies increased when maternal imitation increased. In contrast, Mary's baby's vocalisation rate decreased as the rate of maternal imitation decreased.

Mothers selected for the Parent–Child Interaction Programme had been assessed as having the basic skills necessary to physically care for their children. Being able to meet the basic physical and safety needs of the child is essential however, many of the other mothers also could have benefited from the parent-child interaction intervention.

# CHAPTER 11

# Lessons for Practice

Five behavioural parent education programmes focussing on prevention of child neglect were developed with and for young vulnerable mothers and their babies. The programmes were conducted in a residential assessment centre that offered separate flats for each mother-baby dyad, a common area for all residents, and relatively high levels of staff supervision. Lessons from the research and development of these programmes are outlined in this chapter. This is not a 'cookbook' approach, where practitioners can take 'recipes' or set programmes and apply them blindly to diverse settings and different families: instead lessons are distilled from research on how to apply the general approach of behaviour analysis to child neglect prevention, and require knowledgeable flexibility and a science-based, inquisitive approach from professionals so that the programmes are adapted and tailored to each individually family.

The programmes were designed specifically to increase parental skills in areas of child care that, when omitted, were linked directly to child neglect. The target behaviours were identified as key skills necessary for adequate child care that are commonly experienced as difficult by young mothers themselves; these included child care skills, child care routines, home safety, home hygiene, and mother-child interaction.

## Review of programmes

The first programme focussed on increasing parental skills that are needed for the basic physical care of children. Skills included in this programme were bathing and feeding the baby. Seven mothers participated in the development of the programme. Results for bathing showed that bathing skills improved for all mothers and were maintained at or above criterion levels. Feeding skills training had less defined results; feeding skills of all mothers reached criterion levels, however progress was only maintained by two mothers. It became apparent that mothers who had difficulty with feeding skills had problems maintaining routines, therefore the second programme focussed on developing child care routines. These mothers also often failed to talk to or look at their babies during feeding, an issue addressed later, in Chapter 10 through the Parent Child Interaction Programme.

The emphasis of the second programme was on child care routines, in particular the planning of and adherence to routines. This intervention helped mothers to create a stable and predictable environment for their children. Three mothers participated in this programme and results showed that all mothers were able to plan routines for their child care tasks, but had problems adhering to their plans. The main difficulty in managing routines was that other activities, particularly those involving social contact, took priority over planned child care tasks. This programme showed that the interaction between mother and baby was not reinforcing caregiving behaviour for these mothers, an issue that was addressed in Chapter 10, where the focus was on mother-child interaction.

Home safety and home hygiene were issues that posed considerable dangers to young babies and toddlers. Therefore, the third programme entailed the development and implementation of a parent education programme to improve skills to ensure safety in the home. A checklist for dangers in the home was developed and combined with advice on developmental expectations of children and child supervision. Reinforcement contingencies were designed to increase the home safety skills of the mothers. Four mothers participated in this programme; two of the mothers had two children, the other two mothers had one child each. Results showed that the intervention was effective in reducing the number of dangers in the home. Supervision of the children to ensure that they were safe emerged as a key component of this programme. The difficulties lone parents can have in providing adequate levels of supervision was especially pertinent for young parents who had more than one very young child. Collaboration with child care facilities, such as nurseries was important to allow for respite time for the mothers so they could ensure physical home safety by tidying up the flat without neglecting the supervision needs of the children.

The fourth programme described the development of an intervention to improve levels of hygiene in the home. Adequate levels of home hygiene are particularly important for very young babies who can get very ill in unhygienic, infection-prone environments. Five mothers participated in this programme and learned the necessary skills to maintain their homes in a clean and hygienic condition. Results showed that all mothers were able to reach criterion levels during intervention; however, none of the gains were maintained during follow-up. The mothers who had the lowest scores overall also had difficulties in other areas of child care. Home hygiene emerged as a key indicator and benchmark for child neglect.

The final programme focussed on strategies to enrich the frequency and quality of mother-child interaction by focussing on the parental skills of recognising and responding to their babies' cues. Earlier chapters on child care skills had identified the importance of mother-child interactions as a basis for other child care. The previous programmes showed that mothers were able to learn child care skills but were not able to maintain these without good mother-child interactions. Clearly, if child responses and wellbeing do not function as reinforcers for the development and maintenance of parental child care behaviours, the probability of these behaviours remains low and the likelihood of neglect rises. Three mothers participated in this programme. Results showed that one mother was able to reach and maintain criterion levels during intervention. The second mother made little progress with any of the target behaviours. The third mother made good progress in all target behaviours, but withdrew from the procedure before follow-up data could be collected. This programme highlighted the importance not only of skills levels but also of sensitivity in the interaction. Mother-child interaction and the quality of this interaction emerged as second key indicator and benchmark for child neglect.

Overall, results show that programmes were effective when the mother's difficulties were caused by a skills deficit directly related to the specific child care task but less so when mothers had the necessary skills, but were distracted from the task by other events. Skills that were related directly to the baby's immediate needs or cues, such as feeding, routines, or interaction were more challenging for some mothers than tasks that could be performed at times selected by mothers, such as bathing the baby or cleaning the flat.

While the practice tools developed in these programmes provide valuable assessment instruments for child care workers some of the most important lessons relate to the empirical approach taken in the development and evaluation of the programmes. Child care workers who use the intra-system approach adopted in these programmes, in other words, who use single-system designs to collect objective behavioural data, will be able not only to monitor the effect of the programmes instantaneously across time, but more importantly they will be able to adjust the programmes to the individual needs of the families.

## Outcomes for families

Nine of the families achieved Optimal Outcome, where the mother and child together moved into independent housing in the community. Table 11.1 shows the background, programmes, and outcomes for these families. Despite the fact that some of the mothers had intellectual disabilities and all participating children were considered at high risk of neglect prior to intervention, these parents were able to learn the skills necessary for adequate child care. For many of these families this was a difficult and time-consuming process, however for the most part, newly learned child care skills were maintained. For some of the families, maintenance data were missing because the family moved into the community before data collection was completed. The key for all of these Optimal Outcomes families was social support.

Arguably, six of the families reached Low Outcomes where the children did not remain in the care of their mothers. Table 11.2 shows the background, programmes, and outcomes for these families. In three cases, the children were freed for adoption and in the other three families the children were placed in long-term foster care with a view to being freed for adoption. This means that despite taking part in detailed and focussed parent education programmes, in 40% of cases the children were eventually adopted. Although this figure is high, it is important to remember that without admission to the project and behaviour parent education intervention all of these children would likely have ended up in the care system, where only about 1/3 of all children ultimately are placed in stable foster or adoption families.

Adoption, Freeing, Placement, or Permanency Orders are legal procedures that differ

**Table 11.1:** Optimal Outcome families: background, interventions, and outcomes

| Name | Age | Learning difficulty | Social support | Skills trained | Skills maintained | Placement outcome |
|---|---|---|---|---|---|---|
| Laura | 16 | N | Y | Bathing | Y | Family in community |
| Evelyn | 24 | Y | Y | Bathing | Y | Family in community |
|  |  |  |  | Interaction | Y |  |
| Jane | 16 | N | Y | Feeding | Y | Family in community |
| Lee | 21 | Y | Y | Feeding | Y | Family in community |
| Judy | 19 | N | Y | Safety | Y | Family in community |
| Lynne | 17 | N | Y | Safety | N | Family in community |
| Karen | 20 | Y | Y | Safety | Y | Family in community |
|  |  |  |  | Hygiene | N |  |
| Hannah | 17 | N | Y | Hygiene | N | Family in community |
| Alice | 18 | N | Y | Interaction | Y | Family in community |

**Table 11.2:** Low Outcome families: background, intervention, and outcomes

| Name | Age | Learning difficulty | Social support | Skills trained | Skills maintained | Placement outcome |
|---|---|---|---|---|---|---|
| Charlotte | 18 | N | N | Feeding | N | Freeing order Adoption |
| Ruby | 25 | N | N | Bathing | Y | Freeing order |
|  |  |  |  | Feeding | N | Adoption |
|  |  |  |  | Routines | N |  |
|  |  |  |  | Hygiene | N |  |
| Susan | 17 | N | N | Routines | N | Freeing order |
|  |  |  |  | Hygiene | N | Adoption |
| Caroline | 16 | N | N | Bathing | Y | State care |
|  |  |  |  | Feeding | N |  |
|  |  |  |  | Routines | N |  |
| Cathleen | 19 | N | N | Safety | Y | State care |
|  |  |  |  | Hygiene | N |  |
| Mary | 18 | N | N | Interaction | N | State care |

procedurally and in name across jurisdictions but all have the same outcome: they remove parental rights of the birth parent and place the child with adoptive parents who gain full parental rights and responsibilities. Neglect or high risk of neglect (80%) and birth mothers in care (50%) are the most common reason for adoption (Kelly & McSherry, 2001). In approximately 3/4 of cases adoption is contested, yet in 94% of contested cases Freeing Orders are legally granted. An indication of the severity of problems present in some of the families who took part in the programmes is the fact that in Northern Ireland with a total population of approx. 1.6 million people, the High Court Judge disposes only approximately 12 Freeing Orders per year (Judicial Statistics, 2011).

In children's services, all children are considered vulnerable because of their level of support need and dependency, however the children included in the programmes were particularly vulnerable because many of their parents had grown up in State care, had little or no experience with good parenting themselves, and had experienced abuse and neglect themselves. The effect on the children of the lack of quality care provided by their mothers was clearly evident. Some children showed physical effects of neglect, for example, repeated diarrhoea or poor weight gain that would have serious long-term consequences. In the project, of course child care staff ensured that the children's physical needs were met, and where mothers did not learn the necessary skills despite the programmes the children were taken into care or freed for adoption, where their condition improved rapidly. In general, the babies and children of mothers for whom the programmes were more successful presented as contented, responsive, meeting all their developmental milestones. Children whose mothers were emotionally or physically unavailable and who therefore received inconsistent care, became passive and difficult to engage during interaction with any adult.

## Key features of the programmes

The programmes had a number of key features. First and foremost, they were firmly based on behaviour analytic principles, which included the application of specific learning principles to individually tailor interventions in collaboration with participants to ensure social validity. Furthermore, each programme began with clear behavioural definitions and repeated measurements of specific behavioural dimensions across time and included carefully planned reinforcement contingencies for the establishment, generalisation and maintenance of target behaviours.

## Behaviour analytic principles

There are many behavioural principles that have been discovered by behaviour analysts over the years. The word 'discovered' is important here, because behaviour analytic principles were not 'invented' or 'designed' by specific theorists, they were discovered through careful scientific experimentation, initially in the laboratory and eventually in real life settings. The main behavioural principles used in the behavioural parent education programmes were reinforcement contingencies; staff and peer in-vivo modelling; video modelling and feedback; and written and verbal instructions. Punishment contingencies were avoided as they commonly have many undesired side effects (Dillenburger & Keenan, 1994).

Modelling and imitation was used frequently throughout the programmes. Modelling may have been more effective if models that were similar to mothers had been available. Video modelling was a useful tool for teaching mothers to respond sensitively to the baby's cues; mothers were filmed carrying out child care tasks and were therefore able to receive constructive feedback and act as their own models.

## Individually tailored interventions

Behaviour analytic interventions typically are individually tailored (Keenan & Dillenburger, 2011). This means that the programmes were carefully tailored to the needs of each child and each parent. A full range of factors were taken into account including biological factors, such as physical, sensory, or intellectual disabilities; the developmental level and past learning history of the child; the present circumstances and contingencies for the mother; as well as the cultural norms of the family. These factors dictated which interventions were developed for which family, for example, the Home Safety Programme was not necessary for mothers of very young babies until they were mobile and able to move around the flat unaided. Importantly, the programmes helped mothers to understand developmental milestones and trajectories. As such mothers were encouraged to ensure that interventions were tailored around their child's individual needs; for example, child care routines were based on each child's normal daily rhythms that were identified by their mothers rather than being based on preconceived ideas about how a routine should be followed.

A good example of the need to individually tailor programmes was the changing level of adult supervision necessary as the children achieved different 'developmental cusps' (Rosales-Ruiz & Baer, 1997). A developmental cusp is defined pragmatically as a behaviour or class of behaviours that allows access to new, previously inaccessible reinforcers leading to further behavioural development. Behavioural cusps have been identified as useful developmental target behaviours (Bosch & Fuqua, 2001).

As the children acquired new developmental cusps, for example, learned to crawl or walk, different levels of supervision were needed and the difficulties of supervising more than one very young child were highlighted in the home safety programme. Toddlers who were more mobile than very young babies were particularly at risk of accidental injury in cases of poor parental supervision. Unlike child care tasks, such as feeding or changing a nappy, that take a specified amount of time before they need to be carried out again, supervision for young children needed to be constant during waking hours and most mothers learned about appropriate levels of supervision through a combination of education and experience. Others were provided with a nursery place for their children that allowed them time to complete household tasks, such as cleaning, making the home safe, or preparing meals for the baby. Some of the mothers did not appear to learn through experience, even though their children suffered repeated minor injuries due to lack of supervision.

Of course, individually tailored intervention principles also applied to the mothers. Staff ensured that the methods used in the interventions were easily understood by mothers and provided a transparent way of communicating with the families. As the content of each procedure was agreed with mothers, they were clear about expectations and about the basis on which decisions were made. Staff feedback was constructive and linked to specific behaviours, rather than being a generic criticism of the mother.

## Collaboration with participants and achieving social validity

Each programme focussed on different areas of child care and obviously not all components within a programme were automatically relevant for each family. To ensure ethnically sensitive and anti-oppressive practice, parents were fully involved, starting with the identification of acceptable standards of child care and target behaviours right through to ensuring that improvements were maintained following discharge from the project. Recording sheets for Routines, Home Safety and Home Hygiene were completed jointly between mothers and project staff. As the content of each procedure was agreed with mothers, they were clear about expectations and about the basis on which decisions were made. Interventions were easily understood and provided a transparent way of communicating with the families and staff feedback was constructive and linked to specific behaviours, rather than being a generic criticism of the mother.

Sharing responsibility with mothers also increased the chances of skills being generalised across to other staff members, especially when mothers were exposed to distracting influences of friends or families or experienced personal difficulties, such as stress, depression or social isolation. More on this later.

Jointly selecting appropriate intervention goals, procedures, and outcomes enhanced the social validity of the programmes, as even mothers who did not meet all the targets of acceptable and safe

practices, had no problem in identifying social validity criteria for their own families.

Staff members also were fully included in the design of the programmes, which meant that they too were confident about using the procedures. This was important in particular because working with families where neglect is an issue can be stressful, engendering feelings of helplessness, being overwhelmed, and burnout (Dillenburger, 2004). It also meant that training staff to competently implement the procedures was relatively straightforward. For most of the procedures only one training session was required, which included:

- An introduction to the assessment programme.
- Direct teaching, practice exercises, discussion and a written test on basic behavioural principles and on using single case designs.
- Examples and discussion of the routine procedure.
- Practice scoring of checklists on video for basic child care skills, and interaction.
- Live scoring in specifically arranged flats, for home safety and hygiene.

## Behavioural definitions

Behavioural programmes generally start with an agreement between participants and staff regarding the definition of target behaviours. Programmes that focus on child neglect are no different; however the problem is that neglect is the omission of appropriate parenting behaviours, rather than the commission of abusive behaviours. Defining target behaviours therefore depends on a definition of what constitutes inappropriate versus good or at least appropriate parenting behaviours. There are no universally agreed appropriate parenting behaviours and a further complication is the fact that a wide range of behaviours can result in neglect that are not directly related to child care, for example, alcohol or substance misuse. Other factors, such as poverty and unemployment as well as the age and developmental needs of the child play a major part in the identification of crucial parenting behaviours.

Where standards were not set directly in collaboration with the mothers, for example, in the standard assessment checklists used in the first programme, were based on observations of other mothers in the project and participating mothers agreed to the target behaviours before they were used. Discussing and agreeing definitions of target behaviours with the mothers meant that they were not being asked to meet standards that were based on the value system of staff but rather on their own ideas of what they could and should achieve.

Although a range of behaviours were targeted, it was impossible to include all behaviour relevant to parenting. However, the results of the programmes gave a picture of the quality of physical and emotional care that the child received. Programmes that involved interaction with the child, either when completing child care tasks or specifically addressing interaction provided a useful benchmark for the overall quality of the mother's relationship with her child.

Neglect, being omission of appropriate rather than commission of inadequate parental behaviours, generally results in a build-up of effects over a period of time, rather than occurring in one major easily identifiable traumatic event. This makes gathering evidence and defining behavioural dimensions difficult. Some of the basic programmes used here were originally designed for mothers with intellectual disabilities (Feldman et al., 1994); however results showed that with minor adjustments, they were applicable to vulnerable mothers who lacked basic child care skills. Using assessment tools within a single-system research paradigm that clearly demonstrate progress or lack thereof offer valuable tools to child care workers who are required to make decisions about the welfare of a child.

## Repeated measurement across time

Once target behaviours were identified, defined, and agreed, single-system research techniques were used to ensure repeated measurement across time, starting with the collection of baseline data followed by on-going review and evaluation. Since observations were conducted in the natural environment of the flat in which these families lived, rather than a clinical setting, a clear picture emerged of the antecedents and consequences that functioned to establish and maintain the target behaviour.

Prior to implementing the programmes at times staff members found it difficult to remain objective as they felt very protective towards the mothers they were working with, in particular those who

were young and vulnerable. This made it difficult to always ensure that the babies' needs were always prioritised over the mothers' needs. Using the checklists provided more objective measures to guide decision-making.

Routines were of central importance because, in order to prevent neglect, most child care tasks have to be undertaken repeatedly and at regular intervals. It is clearly not enough that child care tasks are performed accurately they also have to be completed fluently, in other words, repeatedly at appropriate times and at an adequate pace. The overall wellbeing of children who received unpredictable care was negatively affected. Physical effects included severe nappy rash caused by sporadic nappy changes and infrequent bathing. Unpredictable environments generally have adverse effects on children's development, for example, unsettled behaviour is inadvertently shaped if parental responses were calm one minute and erratic the next.

## Designing contingencies of reinforcement

The focus on contingencies of reinforcement (rather than punishment) made the programmes a positive experience for mothers. A few of the mothers responded well to naturally occurring contingencies, such as their child's responses or developmental progress. These mothers also received on-going verbal praise from project staff and more formal praise from a range of professionals during reviews or case conferences.

For most parents, this did not happen. In fact, for most of the mothers the child's cues did not function as antecedents for child care behaviours nor did the child's responses function to positively reinforce caretaking behaviour. Conditioned reinforcers, such as verbal praise and vouchers were necessary to establish and maintain child care behaviours. Vouchers were used because they could be given immediately following the desired behaviour and later exchanged for a range of more tangible reinforcers: however for some of the mothers, vouchers and praise were only effective in the short term.

In some cases artificially constructed reinforcers were unable to compete with external contingencies, such as social contact with friends, which offered social reinforcement and temporary escape from the assessment process. Mothers who had very low levels of social contact were particularly susceptible to opportunities to socialise. Some mothers had few friends and had difficulty maintaining relationships, which resulted in a limited social network. Friends and family members' contact with mothers was often unreliable and they changed or cancelled arrangements at the last minute. This intermittent schedule of social reinforcement meant that the reinforcers became even stronger for mothers already deprived of social contact.

On the other hand, negative reinforcers functioned to increase some of the child care behaviours that ensured escape or avoidance of aversive consequences, such as disapproval from staff or a crying baby. In extreme cases, the threat of removal of the child from the mother's care resulted in mothers avoiding contact with project staff or field child care worker who in turn frequently interpreted this as a lack of motivation to parent.

Some mothers sought out staff company when their children were not with them or when they were asleep, but avoided contact with staff when completing child care tasks; for example, they fed the babies when project staff were not present or when they themselves were away from the project. In other words, staff presence functioned as a motivating operation that changed the value of a reinforcer and the probability of behaviour occurring.

The residential setting offered opportunities for on-going direct observation and full exploration of contingencies that maintained or competed with child care behaviours. Close working relationships between staff and residents developed and at times it was difficult to separate the effects of programme contingencies from those inherent in other project processes, such as individual keyworker sessions, dealing with issues from the mother's own past, obtaining benefits, or practical support to secure future accommodation. Informal support was offered throughout the day by staff and other residents as required. During the day, project staff visited each family at least every two hours to offer advice and monitor parenting. Despite this high level of support some mothers struggled to meet their children's needs although generally speaking these were the mothers who tended to avoid structured individual work sessions. Mothers who engaged with staff tended to cope best with day-to-day child care.

## Generalisation and maintenance

Child neglect is considered in two very general categories: recent, short-term neglect or long term, chronic neglect. In addition, we found that neglect can take two forms. It can occur when caregivers lack knowledge or skills with regard to necessary child care behaviour and when caregivers are competent in the necessary child care tasks, but for whatever reasons, do not engage in these behaviours, at least not consistently enough to constitute adequate child care, in other words, when child care behaviours are not generalised or maintained.

Neglect that is merely due to lack of child care skills required relatively short-term intervention to teach the necessary skills. This is important because without behavioural parent education minor skills deficits can lead to chronic or long-term neglect, for example early feeding difficulties can develop into relationship problems. However, the important point was that in these cases some relatively simple procedures to teach child care behaviours were necessary but sufficiently effective to prevent neglect.

The second form of neglect was when necessary knowledge and skills existed but were not applied consistently. Specifically tailored generalisation and maintenance procedures were required. A number of generalisation procedures were built into the programmes, for example, interventions took place in the flats at the actual times when each child care task was completed, rather than in a clinic setting. In addition, different members of staff took part in the programmes to ensure generalisation.

Maintenance procedures were included in the programmes to ensure progress made during intervention was maintained. A good relationship with a partner, family member, friend or former foster carer provided on-going practical and emotional support plus additional help in times of stress. The relationships that were reliable and predicable and responded to the needs of both mothers and children were particularly supportive in relation to maintaining newly learned child care skills. In addition, they offered positive role models for child care and positively reinforced the mother's parenting skills.

It is not surprising that social supports had such a positive effect; most mothers have a family and friends support network and share the responsibilities of childrearing with a number of other adults, such as partners or their own parents. However, although many of the mothers in the project had some family contact, this was not necessarily supportive. Many of these young women had been maltreated by their families and could not rely on family support. In fact, the main difference between mothers who benefitted most from the programmes and those who benefitted least was the level of social contact and support. Social isolation was associated with difficulties in accessing supports such as parenting groups that can be important supports for mothers. They can provide models of appropriate child care and offer social reinforcement for adhering to community rules about child care and maintenance of child care skills.

With regards to maintenance of child care behaviours, individual factors such as intellectual disabilities did not hinder progress. In fact, the same standard assessment checklists were used for mothers diagnosed with intellectual disabilities, although the procedures were adapted slightly; for example, staff read out the assessment forms to mothers with literacy problems. The three mothers with intellectual disabilities had good family and professional support, responded well to intervention, and moved into the community with their babies.

## Conclusion and recommendations

Behavioural parent education programmes can be used to prevent neglect in vulnerable families. The programmes reported here were examples of individually tailored interventions based on behaviour analytic principles. They showed that when interventions are based on target behaviours that are clearly defined in collaboration with parents, considered along transparent dimensions, and measured before, during and after the implementation of a programme they can be adjusted and lead to effective protection of babies and young children at risk of neglect.

Where neglect occurs as the result of a skills deficit, the methods used in these programmes can enable parents to care for their children. When problems with child care occur as the result of wider difficulties, it is vital to address these difficulties. It is particularly important that the child's responses function as antecedents/cues and consequences/reinforcers for parental caretaking behaviours and that parents have sufficient social skills to access wider community

social supports without neglecting the child's needs.

The residential setting of the project offered a degree of protection from some of the stresses experienced by these mothers, such as domestic violence. Clearly parent education interventions used in community settings need to address these issues more directly. Residential placements are time-limited. In the case of the project, the average placement lasted four months, so any progress described is of limited duration and linked mainly to the care of very young children. Intervention timescales varied between mothers but generally the programmes were implemented intensely and frequently, sometimes on a daily or weekly basis. Preventing neglect is an urgent business. However of course, mothers who did not maintain progress required longer-term intervention to enable behaviour changes to become established.

Although the majority of parents moved into the community with their children, they continued to face a range of stresses that left them vulnerable to further difficulties in childrearing. As children grow up, the challenges become more complex and families are likely to need support in a range of new areas.

The many children on child protection registers under the category of neglect are registered because of concerns about the mother's ability to protect the child from other family members rather than concerns about standards of day-to-day child care. Having a child on the register ensured that families received support services when they left the project and case conferences ensured that progress was reviewed by a multidisciplinary group of professionals. Although risks to the child were priority, case conferences were also a useful forum for agreeing the range of supports needed by a family.

Children in families facing a number of stresses are at risk of developing behaviour problems. Parent education has a vital role as preventive intervention before these problems emerge. Early intervention addressing parent-child interaction helped parents understand how they influence and shape their child's behaviour and equip parents with the skills needed to address behavioural difficulties at an early stage. An explicit 'bottom-up' approach enables staff and parents to learn about behavioural principles that form the basis for parent education.

It can be difficult to recognise the serious impact neglect can have on children, because the effect of omitted child care behaviours is likely to build up from minor concerns over a period of time. This highlights the need for training for child care workers and other related professional in recognising and dealing with neglect (McKee & Dillenburger, 2010).

## Finally

The programmes described here showed that skills training can enable young mothers to provide care for their children in spite of a range of adverse background factors which made them vulnerable to parenting difficulties. Yet, for some of the mothers, past events and current stressors impacted so destructively that they were prevented from providing adequate child care even with carefully planned parent education.

The application of behavioural methods offers a number of advantages for families and practitioners. First, the emphasis on building strengths through positive reinforcement makes intervention acceptable and socially valid. Second, shared goals and clear working methods promote participation and partnership. Third, the range of environmental factors that shape and maintain behaviour are considered as the main causes of behaviour, thus evading mentalism inherent in blaming individual intentions. A full exploration of these factors pointed towards appropriate intervention strategies and recognised that behaviour can change with the necessary supports.

For child care practitioners who are concerned with preventing child neglect, behaviour analysis emerges as basis for evidence-based interventions that have an empirical base and can be replicated in other settings.

# References

Adams, R. (2003) *Child Care and Empowerment*. 3rd edn. London: Macmillan.

Ainsworth, M. & Wittig, B. (1969) Attachment and Exploratory Behaviour of One Year Olds in a Strange Situation. In Foss, B.M. (Ed.) *Determinants of Infant Behaviour*. London: Methuen.

Ainsworth, M., Bell S. & Stayton, D. (1974) Infant-Mother Attachment and Social Development: 'Socialisation' as a Product of Reciprocal Responsiveness to Signals. In Richard, M.P. (Ed.) *The Integration of a Child Into a Social World*. London: Cambridge University Press.

*Behavior Analyst Certification Board* [BACB] (2012) Retrieved from The Web 05/26/2013 www.Bacb.Com.

Bosch, S. & Fuqua, R.W. (2001) Behavioral Cusps: A Model for Selecting Target Behaviors. *Journal of Applied Behavior Analysis*, 34, 123–5.

Bowlby, J. (1982) *Attachment and Loss: Attachment* (Vol. 1). New York: Basic Books.

British Association of Social Workers [BASW] (2011) *Code of Ethics*. Retrieved from The Web 05/26/2013 www.basw.co.uk/codeofethics/

Centers for Disease Control and Prevention [CDC] (2012) *Injury Centre: Violence Prevention and Child. Maltreatment Prevention*. Retrieved from The Web 12/26/2012 http://www.cdc.gov/violenceprevention/childmaltreatment/index.html

Centers for Disease Control and Prevention [CDC] (2013) *National Health Statistics Reports. Changes in Prevalence of Parent-Reported Autism Spectrum Disorder in School-Aged U.S. Children: 2007 to 2011–2012*. Retrieved from The Web 26/07/2013 www.cdc.gov/nchs/data/nhsr/nhsr065.pdf

Child Accident Prevention Trust (1989) *Basic Principles of Accident Prevention*. London: Child Accident Prevention Trust.

Child Welfare Information Gateway (2012) *Child Abuse and Neglect Fatalities 2010: Statistics and Interventions*. Washington, DC: U.S. Department of Health and Human Services, Children's Bureau.

Cooper, J.O., Heron, T.E. & Heward, W.I. (2007) *Applied Behavior Analysis*. 2nd edn. London: Merrill.

Daniel, B.M. & Taylor, J. (2006) Gender and Child Neglect: Theory, Research and Policy. *Critical Social Policy*, 26, 426–39.

*Data Protection Act* (1998) Retrieved from The Web 05/26/2013 www.legislation.gov.uk/ukpga/1998/29/contents

Depanfilis, D. (2006) *Child Neglect: A Guide for Prevention, Assessment and Intervention*. US Department of Health and Human Services. Retrieved from The Web 12/29/2012 www.childwelfare.gov/pubs/usermanuals/neglect/neglect.pdf

Department of Health (2006) *Our Health, Our Care, Our Say*. Retrieved from The Web 05/26/2013 http://www.official-documents.gov.uk/document/cm67/6737/6737.pdf

Department of Health, Social Servcies and Public Safety [DHSSPS] (2003) *Key Indicators of Personal Social Services for Northern Ireland*. Retrieved from The Web 05/26/2013 www.dhsspsni.gov.uk.

*Diagnostic Statistical Manual 5th Edition.* [DSM-5] (2013) American Psychiatric Association. Retrieved from The Web 01/06/2013 http://www.dsm5.org/pages/default.aspx

Dillenburger, K. (1998) Evidencing Effectiveness: The Use of Single-Case Designs in Child Care Work. In Iwaniec, D. & Pinkerton, J. (Eds.) *Making Research Work: Promoting Child Care Policy and Practice*. Chichester: John Wiley & Sons.

Dillenburger, K. (2000) Bonding. In Davies, M. *Encyclopaedia of Social Work*. Oxford: Blackwell.

Dillenburger, K. (2004) Causes and Alleviation of Occupational Stress in Social Work. *Multi-Disciplinary Journal of Child Care in Practice*, 10, 213–24.

Dillenburger, K. (2010) To Behave or Not to Behave: The 4-D Approach. *Term Talk*, 19: 8–9, Retrieved from The Web 05/22/2013 http://epublishbyus.com/term_talk_issue_19_autumn_201 0/10014027#

Dillenburger, K. & Keenan, M. (1994) The Psychology of Smacking Children: The Dangers of Misguided and Out-Dated Applications of Psychological Principles. *The Irish Psychologist*, 20, 56–8.

Dillenburger, K. & Keenan, M. (1997) Human Development: A Question of Structure and

Function. In Dillenburger, K., O'Reilly, M. & Keenan, M. (Eds.) *Advances in Behaviour Analysis*. Dublin: University College Dublin Press.

Egeland, B., Bosquet, M. & Levy Chung, A. (2002) Continuities and Discontinuities in The Intergenerational Transmission of Child Maltreatment: Implications for Breaking The Cycle of Abuse. In Browne, K., Hanks, H. & Stratton, P. (Eds.) *Early Prediction and Prevention of Child Abuse. A Handbook*. Chichester: John Wiley & Sons.

Family Planning Association [FPA] (2013) *Teenage Pregnancy Factsheet* (August 2010) Retrieved from The Web 04/05/2013 www.fpa.org.uk/professionals/factsheets/teenagepregnancy#lemgqqjbtztodw0h.99

Feldman, M.A. (1994) Parenting Education for Parents With Intellectual Disabilities: A Review of Outcome Studies. *Research in Developmental Disabilities*, 15, 299–332.

Feldman, M.A. (2004) Self-Directed Learning of Child-Care Skills by Parents With Intellectual Disabilities. *Infants & Young Children*, 17, 17–31.

Feldman, M.A. & Case, L. (1993) *Step by Step Child Care: A Manual for Parents and Child-Care Providers*. (Unpublished).

Feldman, M.A., Sparks, B. & Case, L. (1993) The Effectiveness of Home-Based Early Intervention on The Language Development of Children of Mothers With Mental Retardation. *Research in Developmental Disabilities*, 14, 387–408.

Feldman, M.A. et al. (1986) Parent Education Project II. Increasing Stimulating Interactions of Developmentally Handicapped Mothers. *Journal of Applied Behavior Analysis*, 19, 23–37.

Gershater-Molko, R.M., Lutzker, J.R. & Sherman, J.A. (2002) Intervention in Child Neglect: An Applied Behavioral Perspective. *Aggression and Violent Behaviour*, 7, 103–24.

*Graded Care Profile* (2009) Retrieved from The Web 05/06/2013 www.hertssafeguarding.org.uk/adults/files/gcp/gcp_summary_guidance_0213.pdf

Grant, L. & Evans, A. (1994) *Principles of Behavior Analysis*. New York: Harper Collins.

Iwaniec, D. (2004) *Children Who Fail to Thrive: A Practice Guide*. Chichester: John Wiley & Sons.

Iwaniec, D. (2006) *The Emotionally Abused and Neglected Child*. (2nd edn.) Chichester: John Wiley & Sons.

Iwaniec, D., Herbert, M. & Sluckin, A. (2002) Helping Emotionally Abused and Neglected Children and Abusive Carers. In: Browne, K. et al. (Eds.) *Early Prediction and Prevention of Child Abuse: A Handbook*. John Wiley & Sons.

Iwata, B.A. et al. (1994) Toward a Functional Analysis of Self-Injury. *Journal of Applied Behavior Analysis*, 27, 197–209.

Johnston, J.M. & Pennypacker, H.S. (1993) *Strategies and Tactics of Behavioral Research*. Hillsdale, NJ: Lawrence Erlbaum Associates.

*Judicial Statistics* (2011) *Belfast: Statistics and Research*. Northern Ireland: Courts and Tribunals Service.

Keenan, M. (1997) Teaching About Private Events in The Classroom. *Behavior and Social Issues*, 6, 75–84.

Keenan, M. & Dillenburger, K. (2000) Images of Behavior Analylsis: The Shaping Game and The Behavioral Stream. *Behavior and Social Issues*, 10, 19–38.

Keenan, M. & Dillenburger, K. (2011) If All You Have is a Hammer . . . RCTs and Hegemony in Science. *Research in Autism Spectrum Disorders*, 5, 1–13.

Keenan, M. & Dillenburger, K. (2012) *Behaviour Analysis: A Primer*. Ibook. Retrieved from The Web 12/30/2012 https://itunes.apple.com/us/book/behaviour-analysis-a-primer/id564540452?mt=11

Keenan, M. et al. (2003) *Learning to Observe*. [Computer Software]. New York: Insight Media www.celticfringe.me.uk

Kelly. G. & Mcsherry, D. (2001) *Review of The Freeing Order Processes in Northern Ireland*. Belfast: Department of Health, Social Services & Public Safety.

Lindsay, C.J. et al. (2013) The Role of Imitation in Video-Based Interventions for Children With Autism. *Developmental Neurorehabilitation*, Jan 16. [Epub Ahead of Print]

Lindsley, O.R. (1991) Precision Teaching's Unique Legacy From B. F. Skinner. *Journal of Behavioral Education*, 1: 2, 253–66.

Mattaini, M.A. & Thyer, B.A. (1996) *Finding Solutions to Social Problems: Behavioral Strategies for Change*. Washington: American Psychological Association.

McDaniel, B. & Dillenburger, K. (2007) Can Childhood Neglect be Assessed and Prevented Through Parenting Skills Training? *Child Abuse Review*, 16, 120–9.

McGaw. S. (2013) *Parent Assessment Manual Software* [PAMS 3.0]. Pill Creek Publishing. Retrieved from The Web 05/23/2013 www.pamsweb.co.uk/pams3-0.html

McKee, B. & Dillenburger, K. (2010) Child Abuse and Neglect: Training Needs of Student

Teachers. *International Journal of Educational Research*, 48, 320–30.

Michael, J. (1993) Establishing Operations. *The Behavior Analyst*, 16, 191–206.

National Society for The Prevention of Cruelty to Children [NSPCC] (2012) *NSPCC Warns of Child Neglect Crisis as Reports to Its Helpline Double*. Retrieved from The Web 12/26/2012 www.nspcc.org.uk/news-and-views/media-centre/press-releases/2012/12-06-11-neglect-theme-launch/child-neglect-crisis_wdn89914.html

O'Hagan, K. & Dillenburger, K. (1995) *The Abuse of Women Within Child Care Work*. Buckingham: Open University Press.

O'Reilly, D. & Dillenburger, K. (2000) The Development of a High-Intensity Parent Training Programme for The Treatment of Moderate/Severe Child Conduct Problems. *Research on Social Work Practice*, 10, 760–86.

Pavlov, I.P. (1903) *The Experimental Psychology and Psychopathology of Animals*. 14th International Medical Congress. Madrid, Spain.

Radford, L. et al. (2011) *Child Abuse and Neglect in The UK Today*. London: NSPCC.

Rice, C. et al. (1994) It's Like Teaching Your Child to Swim in a Pool of Alligators: Lay Voices and Professional Research on Child Accidents. In Popay, J. & Williams, G. (Eds.) *Researching The People's Health*. London: Routledge.

Rosales-Ruiz, J. & Baer, D.M. (1997) Behavioral Cusps: A Developmental and Pragmatic Concept for Behavior Analysis. *Journal of Applied Behavior Analysis*, 30, 533–44.

Schlinger, H.D. (1995) *A Behavior Analytic View of Child Development*. New York: Plenum.

Sidebotham, P. & Heron, J. (2003) Child Maltreatment in The 'Children of The Nineties': The Role of The Child. *Child Abuse & Neglect*, 27, 337–52.

Sidman, M. (1960) *Tactics of Scientific Research*. Boston: Authors Cooperative.

Sidman, M. (1989) *Coercion and Its Fallout*. Boston: Authors Cooperative.

Simple Steps (2013) *Simple Steps: Autism. The Online Teaching Platform for The Treatment of Autism: Simple But Effective Tools Based on The Science of ABA*. Retrieved from The Web 05/22/2013 www.simplestepsautism.com

Skinner, B.F. (1966) An Operant Analysis of Problem Solving. In Kleinmuntz, B. (Ed.) *Problem Solving: Research, Method and Theory*. New York: Wiley.

Skinner, B.F. (1974) *About Behaviourism*. London: Jonathan Cape.

Tertinger, D., Greene, B.F. & Lutzker, J.R. (1984) Home Safety: Development and Validation of One Component of an Ecobehavioral Treatment Program for Abused and Neglected Children. *Journal of Applied Behavior Analysis*, 17: 2, 159–74.

UNICEF (2012) *United Nations Convention on The Rights of The Child: UNICEF Fact Sheet*. Retrieved from The Web 12/20/2012 http://www.unicef.org/crc/files/rights_overview.pdf

UNICEF (2013) *Millennium Development Goals. 1. Eradicate Extreme Poverty and Hunger*. Retrieved from The Web 01/02/2013 http://www.unicef.org/mdg/poverty.html

Van Houten, R. et al. (1987) *The Right to Effective Behavioral Treatment*. Kalamazoo: Report of The Association for Behavior Analysis Task Force on The Right to Effective Treatment.

Watson-Perczel, M. et al. (1988) Assessment and Modification of Home Cleanliness Among Families Adjudicated for Child Neglect. *Behavior Modification*, 12: 1, 57–81.

# Child Neglect and Behavioural Parent Education

## Practice Tools

Complete with individual data collection instruments and assessment checklists, these adaptable Practice Tools can be used by child care social workers, parent educators, and other professionals committed to safeguarding children from neglect in their work with all parents, including those who may be vulnerable. Academics and policy-makers may also find them useful in developing a behaviour-analytic knowledge base to inform both practice and research.

Important information for anyone wanting to use these Practice Tools

1.  These Practice Tools are copyright and were originally published in *Child Neglect and Behavioural Parent Education* by Benny McDaniel and Karola Dillenburger (RHP, 2014) (ISBN:978-1-905541-91-1) They should not be copied from that or any other publication.

2.  The versions in that book are facsimiles of those used in the authors' own work at the time of publication.

3.  Anyone wanting to use the Practice Tools in their work must not copy them from the book, but instead can obtain FREE ELECTRONIC COPIES in Word and PDF format by emailing Calder Training and Consultancy Ltd at martinccalder@aol.com.

4.  The Practice Tools available from there may have been amended slightly over time to incorporate incremental developments in the authors' practice and feedback received.

5.  The Practice Tools should not be used without full and ongoing reference to the authors' guidance.

6.  The authors' guidance on using the Practice Tools, both those originally published and those subsequently slightly amended, is available in the publication *Child Neglect and Behavioural Parent Education* by Benny McDaniel and Karola Dillenburger, which can be purchased from www.russellhouse.co.uk or bookshops. Neither the guidance nor any other part of the book may be photocopied or scanned for electronic storage or distribution without permission.

7.  The Practice Tools are available from Calder Training and Consultancy in both PDF and Word formats. The Word versions are offered so that they can be adapted for local use, which is an important aspect of their optimal use, as explained in the guidance.

8.  Because of the possibility of the layout of Word files changing slightly if viewed on a different version of Word than the one on which they were created, anyone wanting to use the Word files should refer to the PDF version to understand how the authors intended them.

9.  When the Practice Tools are adapted for local use or amended or distributed in any other way, this page of information and the copyright footer on each page of the Tools should always remain in place and be clearly visible.

10. No part of the Practice Tools, either in the original or adapted versions, may be offered for sale without the express permission of the authors and publisher.

11. Anyone interested in discussing training on addressing neglect and use of these Practice Tools should contact Calder Training and Consultancy Ltd who may be able to assist and who will share inquiries with the authors when appropriate.

# Practice Tool 1
# Basic Child Care Tasks

This exercise can be done as a group or individually and is designed to enable practitioners to break down specific tasks.

*Task Analysis Exercise*

Jane is 16 and an intellectual impairment. She has been out of hospital one week with her new baby Tallulah. Jane has avoided bathing the baby and has asked her neighbour to bath the baby for her.

*Task*
You are trying to increase Jane's confidence and skills in bathing the baby.

Think about the following:

1. What information might you need to help you with this?

2. What would you need to do to make sure any information is suitable for Jane?

3. Imagine you are sitting down with Jane to work out the steps she needs to follow to bath the baby. Write each step on the observation chart provided.

4. What might motivate Jane to follow the steps you have agreed?

5. How might you make sure that Jane can remember the steps when you are not present?

**Task**_____

**Name** _____          **Sheet Number** ____

| | | | | | | |
|---|---|---|---|---|---|---|
| **Date of Observation** | | | | | | |
| **Time of Observation** | | | | | | |
| Phase: **B**aseline, **I**ntervention, **F**ollow-up | | | | | | |
| 1. | | | | | | |
| 2. | | | | | | |
| 3. | | | | | | |
| 4. | | | | | | |
| 5. | | | | | | |
| 6. | | | | | | |
| 7. | | | | | | |
| 8. | | | | | | |
| 9. | | | | | | |
| 10. | | | | | | |
| 11. | | | | | | |
| 12. | | | | | | |
| 13. | | | | | | |
| 14. | | | | | | |
| 15. | | | | | | |
| 16. | | | | | | |
| 17. | | | | | | |
| 18. | | | | | | |
| 19. | | | | | | |
| 20. | | | | | | |
| **Total steps completed without prompts** | | | | | | |
| **% correct** | | | | | | |
| **Staff Initials** | | | | | | |

## Sample Observation Sheets

The sheets below are examples of task analyses; these should be modified to match the age of the child, the needs of the family and any guidance from health professionals. The level of detail needed will depend on the mother's existing skills.

## Bathing 0-2 months

Name _____          Sheet Number _____

| | | | | | | |
|---|---|---|---|---|---|---|
| **Date of Observation** | | | | | | |
| **Time of Observation** | | | | | | |
| Phase: **B**aseline, **I**ntervention, **F**ollow-up | | | | | | |
| 1. Makes sure the room is warm, no less than 22°C. Closes doors and windows to prevent draughts | | | | | | |
| 2. Sets the baby in a safe place | | | | | | |
| 3. Lays out items needed beside bathing area | | | | | | |
| 4. Lays out towel on changing mat | | | | | | |
| 5. Fills bath with cold water first, then hot. Uses 2 inches of water. Mix the water with your hand | | | | | | |
| 6. Tests temperature with elbow /bathing thermometer | | | | | | |
| 7. Undresses baby on top of towel | | | | | | |
| 8. Talks to the baby throughout | | | | | | |
| 9. Wraps the towel around baby's body while washing hair | | | | | | |
| 10. Holds baby over the bath with arm across the back, supporting the head with hand | | | | | | |
| 11. Washes and rinses hair using small amount of baby shampoo (size of 5p) | | | | | | |
| 12. Dries hair | | | | | | |
| 13. Unwraps towel, puts one arm behind baby's back so that the head back rest on the bend of arm. Grips the arm furthest away other arm supporting the legs as baby is lowered into bath | | | | | | |
| 14. While the baby is lying on his back washes his/her front | | | | | | |
| 15. Leans the baby forward over the other arm, still holding his/her arm to wash the back | | | | | | |
| 16. Removes baby from bath and lays on towel | | | | | | |
| 17. Dries baby, paying attention to creases on neck, arms, and top of legs. Dries between toes | | | | | | |
| 18. Applies cream | | | | | | |
| 19. Puts on clean nappy & clothes | | | | | | |
| 20. Sets the baby somewhere safe | | | | | | |
| 21. Empties bath, rinses it out puts other items away | | | | | | |
| 22. Puts used nappy in nappy bin | | | | | | |

| | | | | | |
|---|---|---|---|---|---|
| **Total steps completed without prompts** | | | | | |
| **% correct** | | | | | |
| **Staff Initials** | | | | | |

# Bottle Feeding

**Name** _____          **Sheet Number** ____

| | | Date of Observation | | | | | | | | | | |
|---|---|---|---|---|---|---|---|---|---|---|---|---|
| | | **Date of Observation** | | | | | | | | | | |
| | | **Time of Observation** | | | | | | | | | | |
| | | Phase :Baseline, Intervention, Follow-up | | | | | | | | | | |
| 1 | Puts baby in a safe place | | | | | | | | | | | |
| 2 | Washes hands | | | | | | | | | | | |
| 3 | Makes up bottle from previously boiled kettle | | | | | | | | | | | |
| 4 | Checks temperature of milk by shaking a few drops on wrist | | | | | | | | | | | |
| 5 | Mother seated comfortably holding baby semi-upright, with head rested on mother's elbow | | | | | | | | | | | |
| 6 | Puts on bib | | | | | | | | | | | |
| 7 | Ensures that the bottle is tilted so that the feeding end is full of milk and without air bubbles | | | | | | | | | | | |
| 8 | Stops half way through the feed to check for wind | | | | | | | | | | | |
| 9 | Holds the baby either upright against shoulder, or on mother's knee with baby's chin supported, rubs back gently | | | | | | | | | | | |
| 10 | Gives the remaining milk | | | | | | | | | | | |
| 11 | If the baby refuses the bottle tries winding again and offers bottle again | | | | | | | | | | | |
| 12 | Puts baby in a safe place | | | | | | | | | | | |
| 13 | Discards remaining milk | | | | | | | | | | | |
| 14 | Rinses out bottle | | | | | | | | | | | |
| 15 | Talks to baby and maintains eye contact | | | | | | | | | | | |

| | | | | | | | | | |
|---|---|---|---|---|---|---|---|---|---|
| **Total steps completed without prompts** | | | | | | | | | |
| **% correct** | | | | | | | | | |
| **Staff Initials** | | | | | | | | | |

Comments:

*Child Neglect and Behavioural Parent Education* © Benny McDaniel and Karola Dillenburger 2014
Practice Tools available from www.caldertrainingandconsultancy.co.uk

# Practice Tool 2
# Routines

**Team or individual exercise - Routine**

<u>Background</u>
Lisa is 19 years old and has a 1 year old son, Albert. Lisa has not established any routine for Albert; he is fed at different times every day and often is not in bed until after midnight. This means that on some days he does not get up until almost lunchtime and as result Lisa has frequently missed important appointments for Albert at the GP and baby clinic. After discussion with Lisa, you agree that you will work with her to establish an evening routine. Imagine you are sitting down with Lisa to work out the actions that need to be included in an evening routine, and the times that she will have them done by.

**Task**
You need to work out with a routine plan with Lisa that is suitable for her child.

1. What information would you need to complete this?

2. Write out all the steps involved.

3. What might motivate Lisa to follow the routine?

4. What might help remind Lisa to follow the steps when you are not present?

*Child Neglect and Behavioural Parent Education* © Benny McDaniel and Karola Dillenburger 2014
Practice Tools available from www.caldertrainingandconsultancy.co.uk

# Routine Contract

Name _____                Date _____

Write in the latest time that you will have done things by, and the longest time you will go between tasks. Remember all of these must fit around your baby's needs.

## Task                    Time or Frequency

Feeding              At least every _____ hours

Sterilising          By _____ every day

Checking nappy       At least every _____ hour/s

Changing nappy       At least every _____ hour/s

Play                 For _____ minutes, _____ per day

Bathing              By _____

Bedtime              By _____ at night

Naps                 _____naps _____times per day for_____

I have agreed these standards with _____. They can be re-negotiated by me at any time.

Signed _____        Signed _____
      Parent                                Worker

*Child Neglect and Behavioural Parent Education* © Benny McDaniel and Karola Dillenburger 2014
Practice Tools available from www.caldertrainingandconsultancy.co.uk

# Evening Routine

Week beginning _____

| Task | Time | Wed | Thur | Fri | Sun | Mon | Tues |
|------|------|-----|------|-----|-----|-----|------|
| Feeding baby | 8.00 pm | | | | | | |
| Filling in feeding chart | 8.30 pm | | | | | | |
| Bathing | 7.30 pm | | | | | | |
| Bedtime ( trying to settle baby) | 9.30 pm | | | | | | |
| Tidying Flat | 10.00pm | | | | | | |
| Score - Give one point for each task done by the agreed time | | | | | | | |
| Staff & Mum's initials | | | | | | | |

Weekly total _____ Target score _____

No of vouchers _____

Notes:

# Practice Tool 3
# Home Safety

## Home Safety Checklist

Before using this checklist it is a good idea to practice scoring to ensure that all items included are relevant and make sense. This can be done as a team exercise to ensure consistency of scoring. This checklist should be amended to suit the needs of the family and the type of accommodation they live in. It is also a good idea to include any additional items at a parent identifies.

### Observer Instructions

**Step One**

1.  Before beginning the assessment ask the parent to sign the consent form, check if there are areas where the parent would prefer you not to look.

2.  In order to complete the assessment you will need the Home Safety Checklist, a copy of the definitions, a pen and a tape measure.

3.  Measure the child from eye level to the floor while the child is standing; a child can climb on anything at or below eye level. Measure the child from the tip of the hand to the floor to assess their reach. Both these measurements should be recorded on the top of the sheet so that you can assess what the child can reach/climb on.

4.  For younger babies that are not mobile count an area within one foot of where they normally sit or lie as within one reach. For babies that are crawling consider the floor and low surfaces such as coffee tables or settees within reach.

5.  Assess each room by walking through once in a clockwise direction, scoring 0 if the danger is present and 1 if it is not. If steps do not apply these should not be scored- just mark them N/A

6.  Calculate the percentage by dividing the total score by the maximum possible score (don't forget to subtract any N/A steps)

**Step Two**
Following the initial observation give the mother a list of dangers to remove or fix. Agree a target score for the following observation.

**Step Three**
Complete a further observation. If the dangers have been removed, and the target has been met award the voucher or other reinforcer as agreed. Agree a target score for the following week. Responsibility may be shared, for example helping to acquire safety items like socket guards, or helping to negotiate with the landlord.

**Step Four**
Following completion of the programme agree with the parent that future observations will take place after two, then four weeks to ensure that safety standards have been maintained.

## Definitions

**Doors or gates left open** should be counted if it allows a child access to any hazards, for example medication in the bathroom, or the electricity meter.

**Within reach** is defined as any object which is potentially dangerous and can be reached by a child either when they are on the floor, or climb onto something to reach it. This can be an object in an open space, for example an unlocked cupboard, or with a child proof top which is not closed or is broken. A child can climb onto any surface lower than his/her eye level, this can include objects that are grouped together and can be used as steps. Remember to count items that can be reached by climbing on chairs if the child is big enough and mobile.

It is important to check inside any drawers or cupboards that the child can reach. This should be done with the parent's consent. Take into consideration the mobility of the child, for a pre-mobile baby include only objects that are immediately within reach.

**Sharp objects** include knives, scissors or razors.

**Large toys** are toys which can be climbed on, include the number of toys over 12".

**Baby left unattended on settee** - if a parent moves away so that they cannot reach the baby if they start to fall. Only count this if the child cannot climb down off the settee.

**Hygiene -**
- Used nappies within reach.
- Spilled food.
- Bins within reach.

**Choking** - Note that any jars or containers of small objects should be included. Check for small objects on floors, under tables, in cots, and on reachable surfaces.
- Include dirty ashtrays as any those contain any cigarette butts.
- Small objects are those that fit inside the choke tube.
- Check toys for removable eyes, or pieces less than 1".

**Ingestion -**
- Poisonous cleaning materials include: bleach, disinfectant, all-purpose cleaners, washing up liquid, fabric softeners, washing powder, shoe polish, furniture polish.
- Cosmetics and shampoos include: soap, hair products, creams, nail varnish remover, nail varnish, bubble bath, shower gel, baby preparations including shampoo and bubble bath.
- Containers with child proof locks such as medications or bleach, which have not been closed properly
- Any tablets, medicine or ointments that are within reach.

**Fire/Burns**
- Ashtrays overflowing should be assessed relative to the size of the ashtray- an ashtray should be classed as overflowing if there is more than one layer of cigarette butts.
- A book or box of matches or cigarette lighter.
- Any grease in a grill pan.
- Fire guards should be in included if there is an open fire. If this does not apply score it as n/a and deduct 1 from the maximum possible score

**Electric Shocks**
- Electric cables within reach, or frayed or worn only if they are plugged in.
- Sockets at skirting level that do not have covers on.

# Home Safety Consent Form

This home safety checklist has been designed so that your home will be a safe environment for your child/children. The worker will look at your home using this checklist to help you make sure that your home is safe. It would be helpful if you would stay with the worker while the worker is completing the form.

It is important that the worker can check everywhere that your child is likely to be able to reach. This includes any unlocked cupboards or drawers. Please say if there is anywhere that you don't want to be included.

I have read, or had the above read to me. I agree to this safety check being carried out, but understand that I can change my mind about this at any time.

Signed _____    Date _____
Parent


Signed _____    Date _____
Worker

# Home Safety Checklist

Parent _____

Child _____  Child's eye level _____  Child's reach _____

Date _____

Observer _____

| Location | Living Room | | Kitchen | | Parent's bedroom | | Child's bedroom | | Bathroom | | Hall | | Outside | |
|---|---|---|---|---|---|---|---|---|---|---|---|---|---|---|
| **A. SUPERVISION & FALLS** | No | Yes | No | Yes | No | Yes | No | Yes | No | Yes | No | Yes | No | Yes |
| Door/ gate left open | 1 | 0 | 1 | 0 | 1 | 0 | 1 | 0 | 1 | 0 | 1 | 0 | 1 | 0 |
| Sharp objects in reach | 1 | 0 | 1 | 0 | 1 | 0 | 1 | 0 | 1 | 0 | 1 | 0 | 1 | 0 |
| Fragile ornaments in reach | 1 | 0 | 1 | 0 | 1 | 0 | 1 | 0 | 1 | 0 | 1 | 0 | 1 | 0 |
| Heavy unstable objects in reach | 1 | 0 | 1 | 0 | 1 | 0 | 1 | 0 | 1 | 0 | 1 | 0 | 1 | 0 |
| Baby unsupervised in walker | 1 | 0 | 1 | 0 | 1 | 0 | 1 | 0 | 1 | 0 | 1 | 0 | 1 | 0 |
| Large toys in cot | | | | | 1 | 0 | 1 | 0 | | | | | | |
| Baby left unattended on settee | 1 | 0 | | | | | | | | | | | | |
| Baby in bouncer on raised surface | 1 | 0 | 1 | 0 | 1 | 0 | 1 | 0 | 1 | 0 | 1 | 0 | 1 | 0 |
| **B. HYGIENE** | No | Yes | No | Yes | No | Yes | No | Yes | No | Yes | No | Yes | No | Yes |
| Soiled nappies in reach | 1 | 0 | 1 | 0 | 1 | 0 | 1 | 0 | 1 | 0 | 1 | 0 | 1 | 0 |
| Spilled food within reach | 1 | 0 | 1 | 0 | 1 | 0 | 1 | 0 | 1 | 0 | 1 | 0 | 1 | 0 |
| Open bins within reach | 1 | 0 | 1 | 0 | 1 | 0 | 1 | 0 | 1 | 0 | 1 | 0 | 1 | 0 |
| **C. CHOKING** | No | Yes | No | Yes | No | Yes | No | Yes | No | Yes | No | Yes | No | Yes |
| Dirty Ashtrays in reach | 1 | 0 | 1 | 0 | 1 | 0 | 1 | 0 | 1 | 0 | 1 | 0 | 1 | 0 |
| Small objects in reach | 1 | 0 | 1 | 0 | 1 | 0 | 1 | 0 | 1 | 0 | 1 | 0 | 1 | 0 |
| Toys with removable small parts in reach | 1 | 0 | 1 | 0 | 1 | 0 | 1 | 0 | 1 | 0 | 1 | 0 | 1 | 0 |

| Location | Living Room | | Kitchen | | Parent's bedroom | | Child's bedroom | | Bathroom | | Hall | | Outside | |
|---|---|---|---|---|---|---|---|---|---|---|---|---|---|---|
| **D. INGESTION** | No | Yes | No | Yes | No | Yes | No | Yes | No | Yes | No | Yes | No | Yes |
| Poisonous cleaning materials in reach | 1 | 0 | 1 | 0 | 1 | 0 | 1 | 0 | 1 | 0 | 1 | 0 | 1 | 0 |
| Cosmetics, shampoos etc. in reach | 1 | 0 | 1 | 0 | 1 | 0 | 1 | 0 | 1 | 0 | 1 | 0 | 1 | 0 |
| Medication in reach | 1 | 0 | 1 | 0 | 1 | 0 | 1 | 0 | 1 | 0 | 1 | 0 | 1 | 0 |
| **E. FIRE/BURNS** | No | Yes | No | Yes | No | Yes | No | Yes | No | Yes | No | Yes | No | Yes |
| Lit cigarettes left unattended | 1 | 0 | 1 | 0 | 1 | 0 | 1 | 0 | 1 | 0 | 1 | 0 | 1 | 0 |
| Lighters & matches in reach | 1 | 0 | 1 | 0 | 1 | 0 | 1 | 0 | 1 | 0 | 1 | 0 | 1 | 0 |
| Hot drinks or food in reach | 1 | 0 | 1 | 0 | 1 | 0 | 1 | 0 | 1 | 0 | 1 | 0 | 1 | 0 |
| Ashtrays overflowing | 1 | 0 | 1 | 0 | 1 | 0 | 1 | 0 | 1 | 0 | 1 | 0 | 1 | 0 |
| Fire/heater accessible | 1 | 0 | | | | | | | | | | | | |
| Grease left in grill pan | | | 1 | 0 | | | | | | | | | | |
| **F. ELECTRIC SHOCKS** | No | Yes | No | Yes | No | Yes | No | Yes | No | Yes | No | Yes | No | Yes |
| Cables within reach | 1 | 0 | 1 | 0 | 1 | 0 | 1 | 0 | 1 | 0 | 1 | 0 | 1 | 0 |
| Cables frayed or worn | 1 | 0 | 1 | 0 | 1 | 0 | 1 | 0 | 1 | 0 | 1 | 0 | 1 | 0 |
| Sockets accessible | 1 | 0 | 1 | 0 | 1 | 0 | 1 | 0 | 1 | 0 | 1 | 0 | 1 | 0 |
| **G. SUFFOCATION/ STRANGULATION** | No | Yes | No | Yes | No | Yes | No | Yes | No | Yes | No | Yes | No | Yes |
| Pillows for babies under 1 year | | | | | 1 | 0 | 1 | 0 | | | | | | |
| Belts, laces or string left within reach | 1 | 0 | 1 | 0 | 1 | 0 | 1 | 0 | 1 | 0 | 1 | 0 | 1 | 0 |
| Plastic bags, or balloons within reach | 1 | 0 | 1 | 0 | 1 | 0 | 1 | 0 | 1 | 0 | 1 | 0 | 1 | 0 |
| Dummy tied on sleeping baby | 1 | 0 | | | 1 | 0 | 1 | 0 | 1 | 0 | 1 | 0 | 1 | 0 |

Circle 0 if the danger is present and 1 if the danger is not. Add up the total score for each area and write it below

| Location | Living Room | Kitchen | Parent's bedroom | Child's bedroom | Bathroom | Hall | Outside |
|---|---|---|---|---|---|---|---|
| Total Score | | | | | | | |
| Maximum Possible score (take off any that don't apply) | | | | | | | |

## Home Safety Feedback Sheet

Please let us know what you think about the work that has been undertaken with you about home safety.

Parent's Name _____    Worker _____

1.  Since completing the home hygiene check my home is now much safer

| Strongly Agree | Agree | Neutral | Disagree | Strongly Disagree |
| :---: | :---: | :---: | :---: | :---: |
| 1 | 2 | 3 | 4 | 5 |

2.  I feel better able to identify areas that could be unsafe

| Strongly Agree | Agree | Neutral | Disagree | Strongly Disagree |
| :---: | :---: | :---: | :---: | :---: |
| 1 | 2 | 3 | 4 | 5 |

3.  I felt comfortable when the worker was checking my home

| Strongly Agree | Agree | Neutral | Disagree | Strongly Disagree |
| :---: | :---: | :---: | :---: | :---: |
| 1 | 2 | 3 | 4 | 5 |

4.  From now on I will follow the advice given to keep my home safe

| Strongly Agree | Agree | Neutral | Disagree | Strongly Disagree |
| :---: | :---: | :---: | :---: | :---: |
| 1 | 2 | 3 | 4 | 5 |

5.  I believe that the programme did NOT help me keep my home safe

| Strongly Agree | Agree | Neutral | Disagree | Strongly Disagree |
| :---: | :---: | :---: | :---: | :---: |
| 1 | 2 | 3 | 4 | 5 |

### Please rate the following

|  | Very helpful | Quite helpful | OK | Slightly unhelpful | Very unhelpful |
| --- | --- | --- | --- | --- | --- |
| Worker's explanations |  |  |  |  |  |
| Worker showing me what to do |  |  |  |  |  |
| Practice during sessions |  |  |  |  |  |
| Practice between sessions |  |  |  |  |  |
| Feedback from worker |  |  |  |  |  |

# Practice Tool 4
# Home Hygiene Checklist

## Workers Guide

### Session One

1. Explain that you are going to help the parent to get organised with cleaning the home. Complete the home hygiene checklist, scoring down the page, writing in the total for each room as well as the overall total. With the parent's permission check inside cupboards, cooker, fridge, bed, under cushions on the settee, this will give you a baseline score.

2. Help the parent to clean the area that has the highest score. This is for three reasons:
   a. To pick an area that will show results most quickly
   b. To make sure that she is able to do the cleaning
   c. To make sure the parent has enough cleaning materials, cloths etc.
   If either b or c is a problem show the parent how to do the cleaning, and identify the products the parent needs to buy. It is a good idea to supply these for the first session.

3. If the parent achieves a low score agree that for the following session that the parent will have one of the rooms cleaned or if the score is high agree with the parent to have the whole house cleaned for the following session. Go over the room/s checklist with the parent. This checklist is to help the parent remember what she has to do, you can add anything else that seems important or that the parent identifies. Set a target score for the following session- if the parent has obtained a low score you may need to gradually increase towards the maximum score, if it's fairly high you can probably aim straight for the maximum. Agree with the parent that if she meets the target score for the following session that you will do something fun (like cooking or going shopping) if she has reached the agreed target. It is important to pick something that the parent really wants to do, or it may be more attractive to get you to help with the cleaning for future sessions.

### Session Two

Again complete the home hygiene checklist, ask the parent to complete the target room scoring with you, praise the parents for any cleaning that has been done and offer advice on anything that hasn't been cleaned/ tidied away. Plot the score on the graph. If the target score has been met, praise the parent, and set a target for one of the other rooms- using the relevant graph and checklist. If the target has not been reached spend the session doing the cleaning with the parent rather than the fun activity and reset the target for the following week.

### Following Sessions

Continue as above until all rooms have been completed and maintained for at least two observations- arrange a special activity as a reward once the whole flat/house is up to the agreed standard. Ask the mother to complete the questionnaire below about the effectiveness of the work undertaken.

# Home Hygiene Questionnaire

**Please let us know what you think about the work that has been undertaken with you on home hygiene.**

Name _____          Worker _____

6.  Since completing the home hygiene check my home is now much cleaner

| Strongly Agree | Agree | Neutral | Disagree | Strongly Disagree |
|:---:|:---:|:---:|:---:|:---:|
| 1 | 2 | 3 | 4 | 5 |

7.  I feel better able to identify areas that need to be cleaned

| Strongly Agree | Agree | Neutral | Disagree | Strongly Disagree |
|:---:|:---:|:---:|:---:|:---:|
| 1 | 2 | 3 | 4 | 5 |

8.  I felt comfortable when the worker was checking my home

| Strongly Agree | Agree | Neutral | Disagree | Strongly Disagree |
|:---:|:---:|:---:|:---:|:---:|
| 1 | 2 | 3 | 4 | 5 |

9.  From now on I will follow the advice given to keep my home clean

| Strongly Agree | Agree | Neutral | Disagree | Strongly Disagree |
|:---:|:---:|:---:|:---:|:---:|
| 1 | 2 | 3 | 4 | 5 |

10.  I believe that the programme did NOT help me keep my home clean

| Strongly Agree | Agree | Neutral | Disagree | Strongly Disagree |
|:---:|:---:|:---:|:---:|:---:|
| 1 | 2 | 3 | 4 | 5 |

Please rate the following

| | Very helpful | Quite helpful | OK | Slightly unhelpful | Very unhelpful |
|---|---|---|---|---|---|
| Worker's explanations | | | | | |
| Worker showing me what to do | | | | | |
| Practice during sessions | | | | | |
| Practice between sessions | | | | | |
| Feedback from worker | | | | | |

# Home Hygiene Check

Name _____     Sheet Number____

| | | | | | | | |
|---|---|---|---|---|---|---|---|
| **Date of Observation** | | | | | | | |
| **Time of Observation** | | | | | | | |
| Phase: **B**aseline, **I**ntervention, **F**ollow-up | | | | | | | |

| Area | Task | | | | | | |
|---|---|---|---|---|---|---|---|
| Kitchen | Dishes washed | | | | | | |
| | Sink cleaned | | | | | | |
| | Cooker wiped | | | | | | |
| | Surfaces wiped | | | | | | |
| | Floor free of dirt | | | | | | |
| | Pedal bin emptied | | | | | | |
| Bathroom | Towels are dry/clean & hung up | | | | | | |
| | Basin cleaned | | | | | | |
| | Toilet seat & handle wiped | | | | | | |
| | Bath clean (no tide marks) | | | | | | |
| | Floor dry and free from dirt | | | | | | |
| Living Room | Room tidied and aired | | | | | | |
| | Room dusted | | | | | | |
| | Table & high chair wiped | | | | | | |
| | Floor clear of food/dirt | | | | | | |
| | Toys tidied up | | | | | | |
| | Waste bins emptied | | | | | | |
| Bedrooms | Room aired | | | | | | |
| | Beds made | | | | | | |
| | Clothing tidied away | | | | | | |
| | Toys tidied away | | | | | | |
| | Room dusted | | | | | | |
| | Floor vacuumed | | | | | | |
| | Dirty washing sorted | | | | | | |

| | | | | | | |
|---|---|---|---|---|---|---|
| Total steps completed without prompts | | | | | | |
| % correct | | | | | | |
| Staff Initials | | | | | | |

Comments:

Name _____

Date Started_____

| Kitchen Cleaning Checklist | Tick when it's done ✓ Sessions | | | |
|---|---|---|---|---|
| | 1 | 2 | 3 | 4 |
| Wash dishes | | | | |
| Clean sink | | | | |
| Wipe cooker | | | | |
| Clean work top and tiles | | | | |
| Make sure oven & grill pan are clean | | | | |
| Wipe surfaces | | | | |
| Brush & mop floor | | | | |
| Empty bin | | | | |
| Make sure fridge is not frosted up | | | | |
| Throw out any old food | | | | |

*Child Neglect and Behavioural Parent Education* © Benny McDaniel and Karola Dillenburger 2014
Practice Tools available from www.caldertrainingandconsultancy.co.uk

Name _____

Date Started_____

| Bathroom Cleaning Checklist | Tick when it's done ✓ Sessions | | | |
|---|---|---|---|---|
| | 1 | 2 | 3 | 4 |
| Floor brushed and washed | | | | |
| Clean toilet | | | | |
| Clean wash hand basin | | | | |
| Clean bath | | | | |
| Hang up towels | | | | |
| Clear up any dirty washing | | | | |
| Empty bin | | | | |
| Check tiles/walls are clean | | | | |
| Wipe any ledges/shelves/surfaces | | | | |

# Practice Tool 5 - Parent–Child Interaction

## Worker's Guide

**Initial Session**

Before beginning work familiarise yourself with the communicating with my baby sheets, and the sheet on modelling, rehearsal and feedback.

**Making the Video**

Explain to the parent that you would like to help her to communicate with her child in a way that will help her to help her child's development. Get the parent to sign the video consent form. Agree that once the work has been completed that the parent can have the video. Give the parent a copy of 'Communicating with my baby sheet'.

Ask the parent to play with or talk to her child in her normal way, using the child's own toys. If the baby is unsettled organise to complete the video at another time. Set the video up so that you can see the parent and the baby. You can use a large mirror to help see both faces. Observations should last five minutes. It's important that you don't interact with the parent or baby during observations, explain this to the parent in advance.

**Scoring the video**

Score the video in another room (so you aren't interrupted). When watching the video you should observe for twenty seconds, stop the video, and place a tick in each box if the behaviour occurs during that time. The scores for each line are then added at the end of each line.

**Selecting a target behaviour**

Any of the parent's behaviours that score less than criterion levels (30% for praise and imitation, 80% for the others) will be targeted in turn for intervention, starting with the one with the highest score to ensure success.

Give the parent a copy of the relevant work sheet for each of the target behaviours and complete the exercise outlined with the parent. Watch the video with the parent asking her to watch the target behaviour in particular, looking at the effect of this behaviour on her baby's behaviour. Once you have watched the video ask the parent to practice the target behaviour with you during the session, modelling the behaviour yourself if necessary, offering positive feedback when the parent completes this. If 'parent reads baby' requires intervention, ask the parent to imagine she is saying what the baby is thinking as she watches the video. If the parent has difficulty with this you should model this behaviour.

Make sure that the parent understands why each of the target behaviours is important for the baby's development.

## Following Sessions

Complete a five minute observation, scoring and feedback as outlined above, selecting new behaviours once the target behaviour has reached criterion levels over two observations.

If any behaviours decrease after they have already been selected as target behaviours, go over them again, with the same modelling, rehearsal, and feedback procedure as before as a booster session.

Continue until all behaviours have reached criterion levels.

# Interaction Checklist

Parent _____

Child _____

Observer _____

Date _____

Location _____

Length of observation _____

Baseline ☐

Intervention ☐

Follow up ☐

Target Behaviour:

Sensitivity rating of session

| | 1 | 2 | 3 | 4 | 5 | 6 | 7 | 8 | 9 | 10 | 11 | 12 | 13 | 14 | 15 | total |
|---|---|---|---|---|---|---|---|---|---|---|---|---|---|---|---|---|
| 1. Parent praises child | | | | | | | | | | | | | | | | |
| 2. Parent talks to child | | | | | | | | | | | | | | | | |
| 3. Parent looks at child | | | | | | | | | | | | | | | | |
| 4. Parent imitates child | | | | | | | | | | | | | | | | |
| 5. Parent gives physical affection | | | | | | | | | | | | | | | | |
| 6. Parent reads baby | | | | | | | | | | | | | | | | |
| 7. Child plays | | | | | | | | | | | | | | | | |
| 8. Child vocalises | | | | | | | | | | | | | | | | |
| 9. Child looks at parent | | | | | | | | | | | | | | | | |
| 10. Child positive expression | | | | | | | | | | | | | | | | |

Observations should be made for 20 seconds, stopping the video to record. Place a tick in each column if the behaviour is observed during that observation interval. Write any other comments/ observations on the recording sheet.

## Definitions for Interaction Checklist

1. **Parent praises child-** any comment directed to the child that expresses approval for something the child does.

2. **Parent talks to child-** verbalisations directed at child, in a gentle or playful tone, this does not include any critical comments.

3. **Parent looks at child-** parent faces the child for at least two seconds.

4. **Parent imitates child vocalisation-** parent repeats, approximates or expands any noises that the child makes, within 5 seconds.

5. **Parent gives physical affection-** any hugs, kisses, strokes, or tickles.

6. **Reads the baby-** parent appropriately interprets the baby's state, e.g. you're tired, hungry bored etc. or parent gives the baby an appropriate dialogue e.g. 'you're telling me that you want to play'.

7. **Child plays-** child uses toys for intended purpose, or plays peek-a-boo.

8. **Child vocalises-** any vocal sound coming from the child except crying, burping or screaming.

9. **Child looks at parent-** Child faces and looks at parent for at least 2 seconds.

10. **Child positive expression-** Child's mouth turns up at the corners, either open or closed.

11. **Sensitivity Scale-** see attached sheet.

# Sensitivity Scale[1]

9 Highly sensitive
Mother responds promptly and appropriately to her baby's signals

7 Sensitive
Mother responds promptly and appropriately to her baby's signals, but sometimes becomes distracted and misses the baby's cues.

5 Inconsistently sensitive
Mother is prompt and responsive to infant cues on some occasions, but either inappropriate or slow at other times

3 Insensitive
Mother is inaccessible or misinterprets the baby's signals. Responses are often delayed or inappropriate, but if the baby's mood and activity match the mother's she shows some sensitivity.

1 Highly Insensitive
Mother is geared almost exclusively to her own wishes. Her response to the infants signal is delayed and inappropriate.

---

[1] Ainsworth, M, Bell S, & Stayton, D. (1974). Infant-mother attachment and social development: 'socialisation' as a product of reciprocal responsiveness to signals. In MP Richard (ed.) The Integration of a Child Into a Social World. London: Cambridge University Press.

# Parent's Worksheets

The 'communicating with your baby' worksheet should be given at the beginning of interaction work, the remaining worksheets should be given as each behaviour is targeted in sequence.

# Communicating With Your Baby

You are the most important person in your baby's life. As well as caring for your baby and keeping them safe, you are also your baby's first teacher. By giving lots of time and attention you can help your baby's development and make a strong and healthy relationship.

It's important that you communicate with your baby because:

1. It helps your baby learn to talk
2. It helps your baby's brain development
3. It will make your baby feel safe and loved
4. It will help you to bond with your baby

We would like to do some work with you to help you develop the skills you need to communicate with your baby and help you to learn how your baby communicates with you even before they can speak. We will do this using a video, which will be yours to keep once we have finished this work.

# Talking to Your Baby

Your voice is familiar to your baby even before they are born, and your baby will prefer your voice to anyone else's. Although your baby will not be able to understand what you say for a while, they will enjoy hearing your voice. You can tell your baby what you are doing when you are doing things like changing nappies or else sing songs. Your baby won't mind if you're not a great singer!

Talk to your baby, and make a list of the things they do when they hear your voice

_____

_____

_____

_____

*Child Neglect and Behavioural Parent Education* © Benny McDaniel and Karola Dillenburger 2014
Practice Tools available from www.caldertrainingandconsultancy.co.uk

# Imitating Your Baby

Even before your child uses words they can talk to you. When your baby makes noises, if you copy them it encourages your baby to practice talking.  Getting lots of practice helps your baby's language to develop. It also helps your baby learn about taking turns- you talk- your baby talks-you talk. It's nice for your baby to get a response when they are trying to talk, and it's also nice for you. Babies sometimes copy adult faces, for example raising eyebrows or putting out their tongues- try this and see if your baby copies you.

Make a list of the sounds your baby can make now

_____

_____

_____

_____

_____

Look at this list again in a few weeks to see how much your baby's speech has developed

*Child Neglect and Behavioural Parent Education* © Benny McDaniel and Karola Dillenburger 2014
Practice Tools available from www.caldertrainingandconsultancy.co.uk

# Looking At Your Baby

Even very tiny babies love to look at faces. Your baby particularly likes to look at your face. When your baby is very tiny it's important that your face is close enough so she/he can see you. Looking also shows your baby that you are paying attention.

When your baby has had enough attention they may look away- it's their way of telling you that they need something different- it might be some quiet time, or it might be something more lively or different. It's important to tune into what your baby is telling you as it will make them feel safe and loved.

Take some time to just look at your baby. Write down some of the feelings you have when you look at them.

_____

_____

Write down how you think your baby feels when they look at you. How might you know?

_____

_____

_____

# Praising Your Baby

You can encourage your baby's development by giving lots of praise when they do things like gurgling, smiling or playing with toys. Although your baby is too young to fully understand what you're saying, they will understand that you are pleased by the tone of your voice and the expression on your face. This encourages them to keep practising new things. As your child grows, it is a good idea to praise all the things you want them to do, and make much less fuss about the things you don't want.

Make a list of all the things you can say to praise your baby

_____
_____
_____
_____
_____
_____
_____

# Reading Your Baby

Even though your baby won't be able to use words for a while they can still tell you what they need or want. Your baby does this through:

- Making noises, like cooing or crying
- Facial expressions like smiling or looking surprised
- Gestures like waving their arms and legs

Your baby will give you signals when they want to play or talk to you, and may look away when they have had enough. You should watch closely and see what your baby is trying to tell you as this will make your baby feel safe and loved. It can help to imagine that you can hear your baby's voice- watch the video and see if you can guess what your baby is saying to you.

# Touching Your Baby

Touch is another way of communicating with your baby, it can let them know that you are there and paying attention. Most babies love cuddles, strokes, kisses and tickles, or even just holding your finger. Lots of gentle touch helps build the relationship between you and your baby. It can help your baby feel relaxed and secure. Just like any other sort of attention your baby will let you know when they want more and when they've had enough.

Research on babies has found that touch can really help a baby's health, development and growth.

Make a list of the kind of touch your baby enjoys most

_____

_____

_____

*Child Neglect and Behavioural Parent Education* © Benny McDaniel and Karola Dillenburger 2014
Practice Tools available from www.caldertrainingandconsultancy.co.uk

## Making sure children get 'HELD'

### Ideas and resources to help workers put Hope, Empathy, Love and Dignity at the heart of child protection and support

*By Nicki Weld*

By the author of 'The Three Houses tool: building safety and positive change' in Martin C. Calder's *Contemporary risk assessment in safeguarding children*.

'Not only are we offered concepts and ideas but clear tools and resources which can be drawn on in day to day practice.' *Professor Nigel Parton*.

'Strong and engaging . . . provides invaluable and sophisticated assessment questions for professionals seeking guidance in gaining clarity and depth of understanding.' *Child Abuse Review*.

2009. 978-1-905541-55-3.

# The concerned other
## How to change problematic drug and alcohol users through their family members: a complete manual

*By Phil Harris*

'Introduces, then describes and then provides an intervention-based programme to help family and friends (the concerned others) bring about change in people close to them who are experiencing problems with drugs and/or alcohol ... a welcome addition to the toolkit for working with those affected.' *BJSW*.

'Focuses on what the concerned other can do and provides a very specific tool to do it, providing an overt challenge that awakens us brusquely to the great potential for change that exists within a highly crucial relationship.' *Child Abuse Review*.

'Offers practical help, support and a framework to be used ... comprehensive ... well explained and detailed ... well researched ... highly adaptable ... a useful tool in many settings.' *Addiction Today*.

The 68 pages of copiable material to be found in this 304-page manual (a complete worksheet-based programme) are also available as a FREE PDF to customers who subsequently register their purchase with RHP, using the form in the manual.

2010. 978-1-905541-48-5.

# The concerned other

New theory and the evidence base for changing problematic drug and alcohol users through their family members

*By Phil Harris*

Setting out ideas that have been demonstrated to work in a context of 'payment by results', academic and practitioner Phil Harris sees the concerned other as the person most able to effect change in the user's life, whilst also taking good care of themselves. Here, he presents the thoroughly researched and carefully argued theoretical underpinning of his work with substance users and their families. Containing the text of Part One of the complete manual (see opposite), this book is essential reading for academics, researchers, students, policy-makers.

2010. 978-1-905541-66-9.

# Assessment in child care
## Using and developing frameworks for practice
## SECOND EDITION

*Edited by Martin C. Calder and Simon Hackett*

For frontline workers with responsibility for child protection, safeguarding and family support, this acclaimed book will:
- help them to navigate the expanding complexities of child care assessments
- guide them to deliver better outcomes for children and families
- protect them at a time when legal expectations are high that the latest available evidence is accessed and utilised to inform assessments and care planning.

Experts in their fields, the chapter authors each draw on up-to-date research and integrate it into a body of knowledge that constitutes high levels of established wisdom to produce material whose purpose is to be helpful more than challenging.

Invaluable to practitioners since the first edition was published in 2003, it 'covers all aspects of how to assess, when to assess and what to assess.' *Community Care.*

The book's systematic and focussed access to the knowledge that underpins their work is also of value to researchers, academics and policy-makers, and especially useful to anyone undertaking postgraduate or post-qualifying studies.

It draws on the published literature from many parts of the English-speaking world. While the attention given in some chapters to local legislation and context is greater than in others, the overriding emphasis on enabling the exercise of professional judgement in carefully mapped contexts means that the book is useful in all parts of the world.

'Thanks to the efforts of all the chapter authors, this book is a significant and worthy successor to the first edition.' *Martin C. Calder and Simon Hackett.*

Fully updated, it:
- incorporates responses to all major developments in the field
- gives increased emphasis to the importance of addressing risk
- includes completely new material, for example on working with parents with a learning disability.

2013. 978-1-905541-85-0.